SPIRITUAL ENERGY AND YOU

Your Voyage Through Eternity

by

WALTER E. BROACH,
MLS, MMSC., DMSC.

Phoenix Pathways Publishing

PO Box 284

Broken Arrow, OK 74013

Publishing Services provided by Paper Raven Books LLC

Printed in the United States of America

First Printing, 2024

ISBN Paperback: 979-8-9899508-1-2

ISBN Hardcover: 979-8-9899508-2-9

SPECIAL THANKS

To Ellen Weaver Broach, the outstanding editor of this wonderful book.

OTHER BOOKS BY WALTER

About Spiritual Energy
Spiritual Energy Explained

INTERNET PAGES

https://walterbroach.com
facebook.com/profile.php?id=100089530483022

CONTENTS

FOREWORD

SOME PEOPLE ARE RELIGIOUS, AND SOME PEOPLE ARE spiritual. Some spiritual people say they are religious, and some religious people claim to be spiritual. It can get complicated. This book covers the point of view of spiritual people while intending to be explanatory of and fair to both religious and spiritual people. After all, they both have the same goal, which is to experience love and joy in their afterlife.

The Western world does not widely acknowledge the material in this book. But it will give you a whole new outlook on life. The book explains how you, as a human being, are a spiritual entity walking around on earth with a physical body. It covers multiple subjects, such as the many dimensions in which you may exist, your soul, what it is, and your feelings of gratitude, love, and empathy. It also mentions the certainty of winning the spiritual war between positive and negative energy during your journey through the ages. It is relevant for its information about the spiritual significance and the importance of cooperating with your soul to find happiness, love, and joy. It has nothing to do with any religion, just you and your relationship with the total energy of the Universe.

This book is unique because there are few books about humanity being composed of spirits walking around as people. A major point of view is the idea that since there was only a God in the beginning, everything formed after that time must come from the substance of that God. It will probably upset some people because it will challenge their religious beliefs. Science is slowly developing information that verifies our relationship with spiritual reality. The book covers reincarnation, past life regression, spiritual healing, Reiki, meditation, and other spiritual practices. Humanity has believed that it comprises spirits or angels walking around in physical bodies for thousands of years, but the understanding of this idea has diminished during recent history.

Many people believe we live in a physical reality, but few people ever think about our thoughts, memories, and dreams as spiritual. And few people think about humans as totally spiritual creatures. When you read about it, it will clarify your sense of oneness with the spiritual world. The content ranges from information that is easy to digest to several parts that get a little deep. We intend the book to help people better understand their beliefs and give them interesting points of view to ponder. In the past, people who read my books said they kept them and often referred to them when they had spiritual questions. I want you to use the principles expressed in this book to better understand yourself, strengthen your beliefs, and know how you can improve your life. I want you to leave happy and wanting to come back for more.

CHAPTER 1
YOU ARE SPIRITUAL ENERGY

PEOPLE THINK LITTLE ABOUT THE UNIVERSE BEING A spiritual place. We know we live in the Universe, and many believe we are spiritual beings. Still, few of us think about the Universe as a spiritual entity and human beings as spiritual creatures. When you think about the subject, you realize that since spiritual energy formed the universe, everything in it must also consist of spiritual energy. This Universal energy, also known as God energy, is like stem cells in human beings. A stem cell is a primitive undifferentiated cell from which a variety of other cells develop through the process of cellular differentiation. Universal energy is also called divine, psychic, sacred, subtle, and many other terms. Understanding spiritual energy is important if you feel you are a spiritual person.

In the beginning, there was a spiritual energy we called God, Source, or the Universe. From this base energy, all matter in the Universe developed. Hypothetically, the first energy particles to form were tiny invisible strings, but this is only speculation at the current point in time. Neutrinos, quarks, leptons, and other invisible particles formed from these strings. They were the earliest particles of matter and were invisible to the naked eye. As you read this sentence, trillions of neutrinos stream harmlessly through your body. According to philosophers dating as far back as the Greek philosopher Plato, these spiritual particles contain knowledge. Plato argued that all learning is a form of recalling knowledge from before we were born. In other words, we were born with the innate ability to know stuff and need to remember it. Plato believed that **knowledge is universal**, unchanging, and nonphysical. He also thought knowledge is not perceivable by the physical senses.

Currently, physicists are viewing consciousness as a state of energy that can exist in all matter. In 2014, cosmologist and theoretical physicist Max Tegmark from MIT proposed there is a state of matter—just like a solid, liquid, or gas—in which atoms process information. This process gives rise to subjectivity and, ultimately, consciousness. When this proves true, it will provide background information to prove our souls are the source of our consciousness and an integral part of who we are.

Many people and scientists refuse to consider the Universe as a spiritual entity and believe that we are spiritual beings. My friend, Mrs. Turner from Mississippi, said, "People will believe whatever they want to believe." She was right! We are currently experiencing a period when science is only beginning to consider the Universe as being composed of spiritual energy. Science is also in the early stages of accepting that knowledge is active in every spiritual cell. Over time, the invisible spiritual particles of the early universe formed larger units, such as atoms and molecules. God energy, or, if you will, spiritual energy, created each of these types of matter. The matter units grew larger over many years until stars, worlds, planets, and other physical units formed. They all originated from spiritual energy while developing every conceivable type of matter. All matter, including trees, dirt, skin, bones, bricks, and everything else, is spiritual energy formulated in different ways, with distinct vibrations and unique knowledge.

You Will Live Forever

You are a living spiritual soul, walking around with a physical shell composed of spiritual energy. Spiritual energy is the animating principle or vital force that gives all matter life and consciousness. It is nonmaterial energy. When you think about the words *spirit* and *spiritual*, you can envision many things. Spooky spirits, holy spirits, spirits you drink, and even supernatural evil beings that occasionally become visible. We talk about high-spirited people who become easily agitated and describe others as having beautiful spirits. When the word *spiritual* comes up, it often brings to mind the idea of something good. We see a spiritual person as someone perfect and possibly even saint-like. However, it is difficult for most people to see themselves as spiritual beings. That is because we see the outside layer of skin, which appears solid.

When we look in a mirror, we do not see a spirit. We recognize a person. And when we step on a scale, a number tells us how heavy we are. The weight on the scales and the image in the mirror seem to prove we are physical entities. We quickly conclude we are physical creatures rather than spiritual beings wearing physical bodies. The reality is precisely the opposite. Each of us is a physical entity composed of spiritual energy.

Spiritual energy is everywhere. The food we eat, the water you drink, and the air we breathe are pure spiritual energy. They are just spiritual energy in different configurations vibrating at different rates. It took us thousands and thousands of years to realize that we can be spirits wearing an outer garment called skin. It is logical to understand the reasoning behind our beliefs. Please hold on, as we do our best to make the logic clear, readable, and understandable. As we learn to understand this information, it is much easier to accept our place in our relationship with the entire universe. It will also clarify why many spiritual people speak of God and the Universe as the same.

Atoms, particles, cells, space, and water make up the elements of the human body. These particles communicate with us, our soul, and each other. Every atom had to come from somewhere. Each particle in our body constantly gets replaced by particles in the air we breathe, our food, and the liquid we drink. Each particle has been in the Universe since the dawn of history. They have existed in many other animals, plants, and other entities.

3

There are over 100,000 times more atoms in your body than the number of people who have ever existed on earth. You have the material in your body that could have lived on the moon, in a few trees, grass, and even dinosaur feces. All this particulate matter has been around forever. It merely changes. You will live forever, and you are experiencing varied amounts of change every moment of your life. You are only borrowing your physical framework while you spend time on earth. When your soul leaves your body, your physical parts return to their spiritual composition.

Our Souls Use our Bodies

You are a child of the Universe. Our souls were already in the space-borne gas and dust released during the so-called Big Bang around 13.8 billion years ago. Some particles forming your body could have been vibrating in stars, which exploded in vast cosmic convulsions known as supernovas during the early days of universal expansion. Over millions of years, the clouds of dust and gas joined through the force of gravity. This force would eventually produce stars such as our sun. Planets formed, and finally, the elements that would make the earth came together. The world created the opportunity for our spiritual energy or souls to develop bodies to enjoy during our time on Earth in a new and more exciting spiritual configuration. Our bodies allow our souls to experience physical feelings, activities, challenges, and situations they rarely face in the purely spiritual realm. The earth was here about 16 billion years before plant life emerged. Only about 4,000,000 years ago, the precursors to humankind started showing up. Children like to run and play because it feels good for them. Exercising continues to be pleasurable for many people into adulthood, although many quit exercising before or once they reach adulthood. Simple hugging and touching can give us pleasurable sensations that our souls enjoy. However, it hurts us when touched too hard or in anger. It is natural for our souls to procreate because it can produce powerful feelings of love and joy while bringing other souls into the world to share the human experience.

Dr. Melvin Vopson of the University of Portsmouth in the United Kingdom posited an exciting idea about developing the original expanding universe. He called his hypothesis "the mass-energy-information equivalence." The theory states that information is the fundamental building block of the Universe and has mass. If this is true, it accounts for the missing energy in the Universe, presently called dark matter or dark energy. It brings up the idea that information composes spiritual energy, which is the vital force of the universe. It also points to the notion that our elusive souls are the source of our thoughts. It is commonly believed thought originates in our brains. Our brains are only the hardware our souls use to communicate our thoughts. Our bodies are merely vehicles our souls use to move and communicate with during their stay on Earth.

That information is an essential building block of the Universe that has been around for many years. Even the Bible in John 1:1 says, "In the beginning was the Word..." John Wheeler worked with Niels Bohr in the 1930s. He viewed everything as information and focused on the idea that logic and information are the bedrock of physical theory. Mathematician and engineer Claude Elwood Shannon, the "father of the digital age," claimed in the 1940s that information was an essential building block of the Universe. In 1961, Rolf Landauer predicted that erasing even one bit of information would release a tiny amount of heat. He said this proves that information is more than just a mathematical quantity. It connects information to energy. The understanding that information has mass and destroying it releases heat energy has increased over the years. Scientists are just now studying the idea that knowledge is a substance in matter. They are saying in lay terms that spiritual energy contains knowledge and possibly the ability to think. They just haven't realized that there is a possibility of knowledge and energy being spiritual yet. As far back as the time of Plato, the early Greek philosopher, the concept of innate knowledge was recognized. Innate knowledge explains such things as why dogs, cats, horses, and other animals know how to walk when they are born, and no one must show them how. It explains innate survival instincts, such as why babies know how to suck on a nipple to survive as soon as they are born.

Spiritual Energy is the primary material of the Universe. Some people call the whole of this energy God. This energy has several unique qualities, such as knowledge. Knowledge is the fact or condition to know something. Knowledge is understanding how to achieve one's goals or information arranged in meaningful work patterns. Your thoughts express that knowledge. Your thinking comes directly from your soul, the home of your innate knowledge. Scientists debate the meaning of knowledge just as they debate everything else. Knowledge is anything you know. It does not have to be the truth. For subjects like spirituality, there are always seemingly many points of view.

The terms God, spiritual energy, and Universe are interchangeable. Spiritual energy, also called life force energy, is the power that enables our spiritual self to move our physical body. It is also invisible to the naked eye. It is less dense than the tiniest particles, such as atoms, quarks, and gluons. We also describe this energy as universal stem energy, a vast primary cell from which all other energy cells with specialized functions become generated. It can create stars, planets, little bitty people, fish, and even happy and sad moods. It's possible someone taught you when you were young that God exists everywhere, has knowledge of everything, and is eternal. That may sound like a lot of nonsense to the average adult. But it makes a lot more sense when you look at God as the entire universe rather than some grizzled old man with a beard sitting somewhere in the sky judging people. And modern science is closing in on the truth of that statement.

TIME magazine in 1988 featured the automobile company Volkswagen that invited the bestselling motivational author Wayne W. Dyer to craft "A Letter to the Next Generation," and Dyer included the following rhetorical question aimed at people of the future: **Can you see yourselves as spiritual beings having a human experience, rather than human beings who may be having a spiritual experience?**

Study this statement for a moment, and it becomes self-evident. We are not human beings striving to be spiritual; we are already spiritual beings having a human experience. Think about it. We existed in spiritual form before we were born. We still exist as spiritual creatures. We always will live as spiritual creatures. We are eternal souls.

Our soul is that part of us that thinks, believes, controls our movement, and feels. It existed before our present human life, and it will continue to exist after our current physical life expires. Our soul is where unconditional love, unending forgiveness, compassion, hate, anger, harmony, peace, and joy live. Our soul is a little piece of the Divine, here to experience this life and its lessons. We are genuine, spiritual beings having a human experience.

The Spiritual Point of View

The belief that we are spiritual beings having a human experience is a soul-centered approach to living. In this approach, our daily issues, and problems, including anger, substance abuse, alcohol abuse, depression, love, happiness, etc., have enormous value for us. Being alive is the equivalent of going to school for our spiritual selves. It can also be the equivalent of spending time on a vacation. We learn the feelings our bodies experience during the many endeavors in which our bodies get involved. We discover stuff like how to make ourselves happy or sad. When people say spiritual, some mean religious, but many spiritual people aren't a bit religious. Spirituality is your relationship with the Divine when it manifests in your life. Spiritual people will study anything that deals with the spiritual and question what it says to find their personal truth.

The spiritual point of view is that everything is spiritual in different formulations and in varying vibration rates. It starts with the base spiritual energy known as God, or the Universe, which exists everywhere, is eternal, and has knowledge. This energy continuously vibrates, changes, and flows through everything. When people talk about God, they talk about the core energy that permeates everything. It contains all understanding, will live eternally, creates other spiritual cells, and is continually changing and experiencing everything all cells undergo. You can call this core energy the God cell, a plain old God, or one humongous group of God cells. It is like a tremendous stem cell or a group of stem cells in that all parts of its system can change into different spiritual energy cells. It makes all types of energy.

The first type of cell creates or transforms into cells slightly different from itself. We call this type of energy angels, demons, spiritual guides, or even the breath of life. This type of cell is invisible, eternal, forever evolving, life-giving, and able to experience what goes on around it. Core energy also produces spiritual cells that can develop into anything in the Universe. Many spiritual people claim they are God because they come from the essence of the Universe, which they call God. They are partially correct. They are direct descendants of God and carry a substance from God that has evolved into their very souls. The soul is deeply spiritual and is a link between each individual person and God or the Universe. As mentioned earlier, the first energy level below the God level can be angels or entities that have brought themselves up to vibrate with joy and happiness.

The following is mind-numbing, but it helps clarify understanding of spiritual energy levels. During the last decades, studies in Quantum Mechanics and Quantum Physics have seriously considered the existence of the soul. The soul, described as a body of unknown energy, is coupled to the human body through mutual interaction. Quantum Physics shows that energy is quantized and has discrete values defined as energy levels.

Other universal energy names are Qui, Prana, Ki, Ka, Chi, Xi, Netter, and Isomagnetic energy. Natural energy resources like wind, water, solar, and geothermal are called renewable resources. They come from sources that regenerate after consumption and are continuously available.

The next level below angels would be spirit guides, ghosts, and other entities that go bump in the night. They have a mixture of God but lack the comprehensive knowledge and the ability to bring universal change. However, they can affect others in their immediate area.

The next level of spiritual energy is that of animals, humans, and other creatures that have the physical ability to move of their own accord. They also know how to think, express emotions, communicate with others, move, and feel. This energy level has the base energy of God covered with soul energy similar to that of the angels and a level that empowers them to develop physical properties, such as human bodies. This level of spirituality has first the God level, the angelic level, the spirit level, and then the animal level. The spiritual energy manifested in different organic and inorganic material types is one more level. This level includes silver, gold, dirt, and air. It has the God cell and the quality of knowledge, although not the power of reproduction and self-directed change. They remain what they are and only change when other forces disturb them. They change just like all spiritual energy and are in a relatively static state of spiritual development. There are untold levels of spiritual energy because it permeates everything.

As time goes on, many people will inevitably come out with more complete information about the levels and descriptions of spiritual energy. Science is at the beginning stage of learning about spiritual power. What they have been researching is the life of the Universe. Science says it all started with the Big Bang and will end in one of several ways. The most exciting ending is probably the Big Burst, which will happen before another Big Bang. Astronomers combine observations through telescopes with complex mathematical formulas to develop workable theories about how the Universe originated. Today, NASA, the National Aeronautics and Space Administration, uses the Spitzer Space Telescope and the Hubble Space Telescope to measure the expansion of the Universe. One goal has long been to decide whether the Universe will expand forever or someday stop, turn around, and collapse into the "Big Crunch." There is also another theory that there never was a Big Bang. Hence, all views are speculative at present.

We usually verify everything we report on, but information about what we experienced during the Big Bang has to be speculative because nobody was around to tell us about it. Something supposedly released the energy of the Universe in one instant and started the cycle of growing and shrinking. The Universe swells to become a being of unconditional love and joy and back to being a tiny ball of pure spirit.

According to scientific theory, if we looked at the totality of the Universe one second after the Big Bang, we would see a sea of neutrons, protons, electrons, photons, and neutrinos. We would recognize them as spiritual energy just above or below the base level. Then, we would see the Universe cool off as time went on. The neutrons decayed into protons and electrons or they combined with protons to make deuterium (an isotope of hydrogen). As it continued to cool, the Universe eventually reached the temperature where electrons merged with nuclei to form neutral atoms. The Universe suddenly became transparent when the free electrons developed into neutral atoms. Spiritually speaking, you were alive and fully functional during this time of extreme change. You were alive, but it also introduced you to a new situation. You were going through change, which is one of the fundamental spiritual laws, rules, or tendencies. Can you believe you were a tiny invisible cell of spiritual energy? The foundation of all energy is spirit. Spirit energy is the basis for everything in existence. It continually changes and manifests into different forms of energy and matter.

THOUGHTS

- We are children of the Universe
- We are spirits wearing physical bodies
- Our souls control our minds and movements
- We are just now beginning to understand spiritual energy
- Spiritual energy is the essence of everything
- Science often views spiritual energy as unknown energy
- There are myriad levels of spiritual energy
- Spiritual energy is nonmaterial energy
- Energy and matter are the same

CHAPTER 2
ALL ABOUT SPIRITUAL ENERGY

WE CAN STILL OBSERVE THE AFTERGLOW OF THE BIG BANG, known as cosmic background radiation, today. During that expansion, you were alive and existing in spiritual form. Chances are you don't remember that time because it was such a long time ago. This expansion stage of the universe was evidently disorderly or confusing, like what we go through when we are about to be born as humans. There is also a chance you experienced love, joy, and wisdom. It is hard to know for sure because no one was around in human form to record it. The early expansion of the Universe was also when spiritual energy started separating into different degrees of thickness, vibratory rates, and communication skills in order to interact with the primary God spirit and produce other forms of itself. Science projects this expansion happened about 12 to 14 billion years ago.

NASA uses gravitational waves to find undistorted information from when the Universe began inflating. It still does not recognize there might be a spiritual aspect to it. This inflation slowly caused the gravitational pull to subside and eased the pressures that cause our spiritual energy to experience anger, hate, envy, and similar feelings. People have felt their spiritual aspect of self the entire time they have walked on the earth. They were naturally in touch with their spiritual self in the early years.

We started as tiny creatures that lived and developed from biological cells in the earth's waters. Then we slowly evolved from tiny creatures into mammals that could survive on food we found on land. The next step was learning to walk on two legs and consume meat we could run down or find in a deceased state. As humans, our ancestors first communicated emotionally and spiritually, just as they had done while still spiritual souls. They also communicated with grunting and sounds when they grew vocal cords. Then, they developed different languages in divergent parts of the world. As they became larger mammals, their spiritual souls continued to use their nervous systems to control their physical movements and communication abilities.

Slowly, they separated themselves from their spiritual nature. They could see and touch each other and mistook their physical bodies for who they were. Although they had a solid spiritual nature, they could not figure out they were spiritual, as is often the case today. Often, they thought certain animals were superior spirits and possibly gods. These gods caused good and bad things to happen in their lives. They thought the gods were more powerful than they were, so they must live in the sky or some other place above them. About 4,000 years ago, they started thinking there was only one God. Abraham, the father of the Jewish faith, was supposedly the first person to teach the idea there was only one God.

Religions such as Buddhism, Hinduism, Judaism, and Christianity continued with the idea of one separate God and developed and expanded the idea. The various religions developed rules for how people should act to be accepted by this God and used their rules to control a large part of the world. For the past 30 years, the different faiths have been losing members. By the year 2007, the religious decline had started. Now, more and more people are developing an understanding of spiritual energy and how they relate to it. The idea that we are spiritual is a deep subject. Beginning in 1905, when Einstein revealed that energy and matter were the same, many people started to understand we are spiritual entities wearing physical bodies. During our physical life, we will experience many opportunities for growth. Over the years, many religious and spiritual traditions have viewed everything in the Universe as part of an interconnected energy web. Now science is on the verge of making the same type of claim. In the past 100 to 150 years, energy science has come up with interesting observations about spiritual power. Many scientific ideas maintain everything is energy. These energies have been called soul, spirit, Qui, life force, subtle energy, and other names. Many of these ideas include an element of the unseen, something more than what we see before our eyes.

In the early days, there was no widespread belief about spiritual energy. By the end of the 17th century, Newtonian physics became the cornerstone of science, and scholars and scientists taught we lived in a physical universe. At that time science described a set of physical laws that affect the motion of bodies under the influence of a system of many forces. It described the Universe as a well-run machine or even something like a mechanical clock. Humans were simply called complex machines. Science considered only visible and measurable things as authentic. They labeled the old-fashioned beliefs about the Universe as nonsense and claimed they had nothing to do with the real world.

In the early 1900s, views changed again with the beginnings of quantum physics. This new science claimed that the Universe is a system of energy, and that energy and matter are the same things. Quantum mechanics arose from Max Planck's studies in 1900 about why bodies reflect light. Albert Einstein's 1905 paper gave us a quantum-based theory to explain the photoelectric effect, which says when light strikes materials, it can eject electrons from them. This theory also influenced our idea of energy. The idea was further developed in the mid-1920s by Erwin Schrödinger, Werner Heisenberg, and Max Born. Quantum physics suggests that solid matter does not exist in the Universe. It shows that the Universe is vibrating energy and suggests that atoms make up the totality of our bodies.

Many Metaphysical Ideas Prove to be True

Atoms aren't solid; they contain three subatomic particles: protons, neutrons, and electrons. Protons and neutrons get packed together in the center of the atom. The electrons jump around the outside. The electrons are so fast we never know exactly where they are from one moment to the next. The atoms, which form objects and substances, are perceived as solid. However, 99.99999 percent of space is filled with electrons, other subatomic particles, and fields. New particles constantly flash into existence because of the pressure of vacuum energy. Although it sounds very complicated, it is simply spiritual energy doing what spiritual energy does. It vibrates, thinks, changes, and has feeling. This is you at your very base. This is your soul doing what souls do. According to quantum theory, solid matter isn't substantial. It only feels solid because the particles in atoms speed around so fast and continuously collide with each other that they appear dense.

The energy, which makes you and all other people, is the same energy which composes everything else. That energy makes trees, rocks, the chair you can sit on, your computer, and your tablet. It's all made of the same stuff. It's called energy. Multiple Nobel Prize-winning physicists have repeatedly shown proof that energy is everything. One of them was Niels Bohr, a Danish physicist who made significant contributions to the understanding of quantum theory. Bohr once said, "*If quantum mechanics hasn't profoundly shocked you, you haven't understood it yet. Everything we call real is made of things that cannot be regarded as real.*" Understanding spiritual energy is excruciating, but it gives us documentary evidence for the truth of our spiritual beliefs.

Another exciting bit of knowledge about spiritual energy is about our souls. At least it's exciting for me. I first became interested in souls about 76 years ago when I saw a movie where the hero died at the conclusion, and it showed a little cloud-like formation leaving his body and heading heavenward. Around that time, I became a part of the Catholic community by getting baptized and attending a Catholic school. At that school, I learned we all have souls and if we are good, God will allow us to go to heaven and worship him. I didn't know who God was or where heaven was, and I didn't much care. That little soul, which leaves our body when we drop dead, fascinated me.

While mired in religion, I attended many denominations over the next 60 years. During that time, no one ever explained anything about the soul to me. People just talked about our souls as if everyone knew all about them. I didn't know about them and wanted to know the soul's who, how, why, what, when, and where. I studied every metaphysical (beyond the physical) thing I could find with no success. Albert Einstein said he would conduct 99 unsuccessful experiments before a correct answer suddenly appeared to him. I feel this happened to me in my search for the soul.

I've seen auras since I was a small child. I was psychic when I was little, but was often told, "It's just your imagination." When still in high school, I remember playing with a Ouija board, even though I heard that if I played with the Ouija board, I would open myself up to the chance that an evil spirit would take over my body and I would go to hell. Obviously, I didn't go to hell. At least not yet. As an adult, I gave psychic readings, took part in seances, moved tiny objects with my aura, and did all kinds of so-called woo-woo stuff. I took part in every so-called metaphysical endeavor you can imagine. I did these things not to prove anything, but to see if what I heard about them was true, and they often proved to be true. I stopped doing metaphysical stuff when I gave someone a reading and could only pick up bad vibes. I realized that what people hear in these readings can reinforce their negative ideas about themselves. Now, I only tell people what I feel about them when the feeling is positive. These feelings I get are psychic, but they don't come from any intentional reading. They come when I get an extremely good feeling about someone. Everyone gets these psychic feelings. People often lose these psychic feelings by the age of 10, and it requires years of practice to revive them.

I've researched the mind and where it is, and concluded it is in our soul. Researchers at Queen's University established a method that, for the first time, can detect when one thought ends and another begins, or a new thought enters the brain. "**Dr. Jordan Poppenk** (Psychology) and his master's student, Julie Tseng, devised a way to isolate 'thought worms,' consisting of consecutive moments when a person is focused on the same idea."[1] The length of a thought worm is the time it spends living in the brain. Most people believe thoughts come from our minds, and they do. But no one knows for sure where our mind is. Some scientists say the mind exists only when the brain is alive so that they can work together. Often, when people die and get revived 10 or 15 minutes later, they know what happened when they were supposedly dead. This type of memory shows that the mind is still active when we are dead, that memory must be stored somewhere, and that storage place must be the mind, even though no one knows where it is. I studied where thought comes from and concluded it comes from our soul and that our brain is only the hardware we use to ingest our thoughts. As our souls use our minds and brains to process our thoughts, they also use our bodies to activate our thoughts.

One afternoon, while meditating on something, a relaxed, comfortable, vibratory feeling came over me and throughout my body. I could feel the sensation on the outside of my body and throughout the inside of my body. It was a feeling I had never recognized before. At that time, I suddenly realized I was feeling my soul. After all these years, it was a joyful moment and gave me a feeling of pride I had experienced it. It felt good. It is easy to experience, and I believe more people don't mention it because it is the opposite of what they teach us to think. Some people who read this book will say I have a wild imagination, and others will say I'm crazy, or even an emissary of the devil. As mentioned before, my friend Mrs. Turner said, "People will believe anything they want to." I choose to believe that what I feel

---

1 Neuroscience News, "Discovery of 'Thought Worms' Opens Window to the Mind," Neuroscience News, July 14, 2020, https://neurosciencenews.com/thought-worms-16639/.

around and throughout my body is my soul. I have been able to feel it for years without realizing what it was. As a reader of this material, it is your responsibility to believe whatever you want to believe.

If you can see auras, and many spiritual people can, you can feel what I believe is the soul if you relax and focus on feeling your aura throughout your body, both in the interior and on the exterior. Relax and focus on the outside surface of your arms. You should feel a slight tingling sensation, a sensation of a very slight breeze crossing them. You may even feel a thin cloud of energy rising from the surface of your skin. This energy you feel is your aura and your soul. And instead of the soul being a part of you, your body is what your soul uses while it spends time on Earth.

Quantum theory has helped us understand a great deal of information about spiritual energy, and in the future, I believe scientists will be more and more willing to admit we have souls. One of the most bizarre premises of quantum theory has long fascinated philosophers and physicists alike. It states that the observer affects the observed reality by the very act of watching it. The Weizmann Institute of Science conducted a tightly controlled experiment showing how a beam of electrons is affected by the action of being observed. The investigation revealed that the greater the length of watching, the more significant the observer's influence on what takes place. As reported in *Nature*,[2] the study found that observing quantum phenomena can change the measured result. The 1998 Weizmann experiment is a particularly famous example. It found that the observer's simple act of watching something affects the observed reality. It's like when you feel someone is looking at you. You turn around, and they are looking at you. This strange phenomenon strongly suggests that everything is energy, is connected, and responds to consciousness. The feeling you get is your spiritual self telling you someone is watching you.

2　E. Buks et al., "Dephasing in Electron Interference by a 'Which-Path' Detector," Nature 391, no. 6670 (February 26, 1998): 871–74, https://doi.org/10.1038/36057.

Although this subject is extremely complicated, it helps us to understand how everything is spiritually connected. Quantum physics states that once tiny particles interact, they become entangled. No matter how far apart they are, if scientists change the spin rate of one entangled electron, its partner's spin rate will change along with it. They move simultaneously, and the twin spinning happens instantaneously, even if they're a million light years apart. The universal energy that permeates everything connects them. The entanglement theory stems from Albert Einstein, Max Planck, Werner Heisenberg, and others. American theoretical physicist David Bohm suggests the Universe is composed of an explicit order. The idea of explicit order means that energy makes clear or broadcasts information. Many scientists think the knowledge of the entire universe is held energetically in every single cell. That our body cells have all the knowledge of the Universe is wild to think about, but it makes one believe that mystics may have been on the right path for thousands of years. We are just now making sense of it. Spiritual people often look within to understand whatever situation they face and resolve it lovingly in their minds.

Our minds contain our thoughts, and our thoughts are mostly self-organized memories of information we received at an earlier time. Spiritual people enjoy giving and receiving past life regressions to each other. In a regression session, one person typically asks another person who is in a relaxed, hypnotized, or meditative state about their past lives. Past life regressions are also valuable when doing shadow work, exploring your inner child, getting in touch with your soul, and learning about what you need to do during this lifetime to live in a state of happiness. When people experience past life regressions, they use their minds to go back and tune into information from another time. Regression often helps to eliminate all of one's hurt, guilt, embarrassment, and anger from a previous period. Many people ground themselves before they start their regression. Grounding is simply a process people use to protect themselves from evil spirits they think will invade them during their relaxation time. Some people ground themselves by visualizing a white light surrounding them. Others take measured breaths while feeling a protective shield around them. Still others will hold sage against their body, or hold on to certain minerals that ward off evil spirits. Some people ground themselves, and many don't bother. When you ground yourself, your spiritual energy protects your physical body. You are protecting yourself from the influence of other spiritual energy.

Regression gains importance as people understand that everything we experience affects us. It brings back happy and unhappy memories from past times to work on, learn from, and correct. The topics brought up in a regression session can be interesting or mystifying. Some common examples include stories like the now 36-year-old lady who remembered her life living out west in what now is called Arizona. In that life, she was a worthless man. He worked on different ranches and often got fired after he quit showing up for work because of his drunken binges. He got killed in that lifetime by being shot while drinking in a saloon. She believes she wasn't the target of the shot, but just was sitting at the bar at the wrong time.

Another regression story is about a young man named Mathew whose father gave him several hundred dollars to buy property out west in Texas. The young man, who was only 21, started in New York, and everything was fine until he reached St. Louis, Missouri. In St. Louis, he promptly got mugged, robbed of every cent he had, and left for dead. He didn't die, but the police picked him up and took him to jail as a vagabond. They kept him in prison for several days until they let him loose because they had no reason to keep him any longer. When he was free, he was ashamed to write to his father and ask for help, so he walked around town until he got a job as a dishwasher at a bar. He was broke, didn't have any friends in St. Louis, and was confused about what to do. He enjoyed working in the saloon and soon got a small raise and got promoted to bartender. After about eight years as a bartender, he saved enough money to open his own bar and restaurant. He prospered, married, and had several children. He said the regression session helped him to better understand his present life. He couldn't remember if he ever communicated with his father again and recalled nothing about his mother.

In several regressions, the people remembered the time between their lives. People usually recognize the time between their lives as very peaceful, quiet, and restful. There wasn't much color mentioned and not much activity, but love and joy were abundant. As these are regression stories, there is no way to prove them right or wrong. The value of regressions is that they give the person regressed the opportunity to look at themselves from a different point of view than how they look at their present self. Regressions often provide a person with an explanation of why they are experiencing their present life the way they are. A regression session can be a unique spiritual tool, even though there is no way in the current state of scientific advancement to prove the accuracy of the information gained. Regressed people tap into their buried memories, which are spiritual, to understand their reality.

Many people have had dreams of past lives. They dream about being a hero, a killer, a dance hall girl, a sheriff, or even a wanted criminal. These dreams are much like regression sessions. They allow people to look at their lives and decide what they want to change about them. Being spiritually connected to everything, we constantly receive information that encourages change in our behavior. We can control whether that change is beneficial or harmful by how we react to it. The information we receive in our dreams and regressions allows us to analyze what is going on in our lives and how we can improve how we react to it. Your every thought comes from your soul. The spiritual language is vibratory. When a child is born, it must learn the language spoken by its parents or whoever is raising it. The child soon learns to pay less attention to spiritual language and more attention to whatever human language the surrounding people speak. But the child will sometimes remember past lives. Memories play a tremendous role in our day-to-day decision making while we spend time on earth.

THOUGHTS

- Spiritual life is eternal
- You are an immortal spiritual being
- You are living in this single instant
- Consciousness flows through everything
- Everything is energy
- Energy responds to consciousness
- Stay aware of your actions and the results
- You are responsible for your thoughts and actions
- Memories are spiritual energy

CHAPTER 3
MEMORIES EVOLVE

MEMORY CONTINUOUSLY EVOLVES. INITIAL DETAILS OF an experience take shape in your mind, and then the brain's representation of that information changes. With later reactivations, the memory grows stronger or fainter and takes on unique characteristics. Memories reflect real-world experience, but with varying levels of accuracy to the original experience. The degree to which the memories we form are correct, or easily recalled, depends on a variety of factors from the psychological conditions in which information is first translated into memory, to the manner in which we look for—or are unwittingly prompted—to conjure details from the past.

For years, people believed memories lived in the brain. Because of recent discoveries found through organ transplant research, a slew of scientists changed their minds about where it's stored. There is a plethora of cases where people who received organ transplants had thoughts, feelings, dreams, and food cravings that were foreign to them. After further study, they discovered these foreign thoughts, feelings, etc., came from the cell memories of their organ donors. Very interesting! Today, scientists believe memories exist in the minds of cells all over the body. Logically, there is a "leader" to keep things running smoothly between all cell minds of the body. Where this "leader" mind exists is for anyone to decide.

Since scientists haven't been able to track where thought worms originate, we can logically believe our memories, although stored in the brain, are produced in our soul. They come directly from your spiritual self or your soul, which is your fundamental self. Understanding all memories come from your soul through the mind and brain is essential. You are your soul, which is the essence of you. And you rely on your memory to know how to act in every situation. Everything you ever learn lives in the mind for a period of time.

Every moment of your existence, you are generating thoughts. The average person generates 6,000 thoughts a day. You generate thoughts even if you are sleeping, in a coma, or have passed away. The truth that people die and get revived again after 10 or 15 minutes and know what happened around them when they were dead is proof for many people that thought is spiritual and continues after death.

Your memory guides you through your every activity. You use your memory to bring up your past activities that can help your decisions in every situation. You also use your memory to manifest the type of life you want for yourself. Your memory of experiences holds the information you used to decide what you want to experience in the future.

Spiritually, you communicate vibrationally. Every thought you have goes out to the Universe, cooperating with it to set the next step of your path through eternity. You must express helpful ideas if you want to do well in the future. We live in the present. The only time we are fully alive is now. The past is gone. Whatever happened in the past is over and done. You can no longer change it. You can think about it or remember it with good or bad feelings, but your emotions will be in the present. When you experience a memory, whether it be a good one or an unhappy one, you bring up the activity and re-experience it right now. Bringing up terrible memories over and over can be called a luxury. They cost you way too much, have no real value, and are useless. That's a luxury. That type of luxury is one you don't need. You should learn from unhappy memories and then let them go, only using them occasionally to help you through tough times.

The voice of your memory comes directly from your soul. If you want peace, joy, love, and everything good while on Planet Earth, you need to build up your memory in ways that will help you. Your every thought expresses your soul. When you feel joy or pain, it instantly registers in your memory. You feel the pleasure or pain of your every thought in your physical and spiritual body. Some people might believe they can't change or remove their memories. You don't have to try to change your memories. They change all by themselves. The memories will eventually go away, anyway. You can get rid of them faster by learning to relax and change them to be less malicious. If you have cancer in your body, you cut it out. If you have diseased memories in your thoughts, it is perfectly all right to remove them and replace them with new, healthy ones.

However, memories are complex. People think of their memory as a perfect record of past behavior, but they are often wrong. Memory is never permanent. They are subject to change, malleable, and unreliable. Events move from your mind to your brain's temporary memory to your permanent memory while you sleep. The journey, however, isn't always perfect. Parts of the memory can get lost or distorted.

When you focus on negative things like stealing, cheating, hurting others, and taking advantage of others, you are liable to do them or have them done to you. A perfect example is the number of preachers who preach about the sins of fornication and then get outed for cheating on their wives. You focus on having love and joy in your life and are liable to end up with love and happiness. People say they want all those good things but can't get them. Their thoughts of love and joy get counterbalanced by their different subconscious thoughts that nullify them.

Memory is pliable and changes with every life and every event we experience. It is as if our memory cells have only so much room to hold information. As they fill up, our duller and less important memories fade away. False memories aren't rare. Everyone has them. Most false memories are harmless. They don't threaten to harm anyone. Your memories are the reality in which you, as your soul, exist in the present.

False memories seem real but aren't. We fabricate them in part or whole. An example of a false memory is believing that you paid the electric bill for your house only to find out that you didn't pay it on the next billing date. Another example of false memory is believing you bought your spouse a birthday gift only to find on their birthday that you didn't. Most false memories aren't harmful or even malicious. They are shifts or tricks that don't align with actual events. Sometimes they have significant consequences, as in legal or court cases where false memories convict or release someone by mistake.

One slight error in the memory process can start the false memory. You can develop a false memory by answering questions about whatever it is. Someone might ask you if the football team wore red helmets. You answer yes, but reverse your thought and say they were black when they were silver. Your memory started wrong and remained wrong, only differently. Your false memory can continue when someone corrects you with the knowledge the helmets were silver, and you continue to believe they were black.

Someone can give you misinformation about an event, and you believe it. You can think a politician is the most honest person on earth, only to find out they lied about everything they ever said. My friend Andrew, who worked for a government agency, experienced malicious targeting when a disgruntled employee spread lies about him. The disgruntled employee told a friend about Andrew's awful behavior and that he needed to get fired. He possibly wanted Andrew's job. The disgruntled employee and his friend wrote letters to Andrew's board of directors, accusing Andrew of supposedly dishonest actions. The only information the friend had about Andrew came from the disgruntled employee. The employee's lies got the better of him because seven months later, he got fired because they caught him doing the same things he accused Andrew of doing. This employee not only gave Andrew memories to remember but also helped create opportunities for others to learn something from the true and false information they received.

Gaps in your memory will often get filled in later with self-created ideas. You might combine elements of different events into one, so it gets jumbled and forms a memory of just one occasion. The emotions you feel at the start of the memory can significantly affect what and how it exists in your memory. Negative emotions lead to more false memories than positive or neutral ones.

It Is All Right to Change Your Memories

You can remove or confuse your memories through meditation, relaxation techniques, and substituting different activities. Say you have an older sibling who used to abuse you and beat the tar out of you every chance they could while you were children. Every time the memory comes up, you can visualize yourself beating the tar out of them or possibly immobilizing them. It is easier if you ever got a decent smack on them. Even if you didn't, you could make up a scene of you whopping up on them. The constant repetition will change or confuse the memory to cause it to lose its sting. You can also use past life regression and present life regression. You give your soul more power when you change or improve your memory. It is like going to a gym to build up your physical muscles. The more you do it, the easier it gets and the more benefit you get from it.

You don't have to change your memories. They change all by themselves. All memories eventually go away. You can get rid of your bad ones by relaxing and changing them to be less malicious. Shadow work, the exposure of your inner child, also helps. Unhappy memories do not belong to anyone else, and you are the person they affect. You can remove or confuse them through meditation, relaxation techniques, and substituting different activities.

By improving your memory, you give your soul more power. It is like going to a gym to build up your physical muscles. The more you do it, the easier it gets and the more benefit you get from it. Every thought you have goes out to the Universe, cooperating with it to set the next step of your path through eternity. You must express helpful ideas if you want to do well in the future. We live in the present. The only time we are fully alive is in the present. The past is gone. Whatever happened in the past is over and done. You can no longer change it. You can think about it or remember it with good or bad feelings, but your emotions will be in the present. Now is the time to focus on developing a better physical side of life for yourself and raising your understanding of how to project love, joy, and harmony.

We have physical bodies for our souls to use. They help us make things, build things, and play with things. They help us procreate, giving us more souls with whom we can enjoy our time on earth. It feels good to hug, caress, and touch each other with gentle love. It hurts when we bash each other with our fists or other blunt weapons. We are only at the threshold of learning how wonderful it is to focus on doing acts of love and joy for each other. When we finally learn to spread the feelings of love and happiness around, the earth will become a place where spirits can come to experience an area of Nirvana. Your thoughts and memories are the real you. Listen to them and do everything you can to change, use, confuse, or forget those experiences that don't elevate your spiritual energy or help you improve your physical life. Memory is basic for our ability to grow in wisdom.

You and your thoughts are inseparable. They travel with you wherever you go, whatever you are, and however you feel. Memories also change during our transition from dimension to dimension between active lives. They speak to you in whatever language you use in everyday life. Say you live in America right now and talk and think in English. You pass away and reincarnate in Mexico. Then you will think and speak Spanish. You may or may not remember speaking English during your life in Mexico. Your thoughts are always with you and decide what your feelings, decisions, and reactions to the events around you will be. Your body is a servant of your thoughts, which come from your soul.

The idea of reincarnation on Earth is exciting and believed by millions. The belief in reincarnation is widespread in India. In America, they may laugh you at if you tell someone you are a reincarnation of someone. Millions of children have memories of their past lives. Many of the stories they tell are correct, but there is no way to prove they have not come from something the children overheard or just guessed. Small children tell their parents about their past lives only to be pooh-poohed. Pooh-poohed is short for being laughed at or criticized for having a powerful imagination. When these children reach adulthood, they forget their memories of past lives. Whether or not they remember them, these memories affect their life path while they are children. They function as a model to show the child how to behave while they remember them.

You can also use past life regression and this life regression to heal. When hurtful memories intrude on your thoughts, ask yourself why you are punishing yourself by suffering from what someone else did. Your suffering exemplifies a person who takes poison to punish themselves for the sins of others. It doesn't help anything or anyone. Admit to yourself that it isn't brilliant to suffer for the instigator of your unhappiness. Forgive them the best you can because they can no longer abuse you, and it is not your responsibility to suffer for their misdeeds. And what they did to you was indeed a misdeed. Give them their freedom and be relieved that their feelings are not your responsibility anymore. You now have the freedom to become the wonderful being you are by evolving spiritually.

My friend Sharon had horrible memories of her ex-husband. Whenever thoughts about her ex-husband came up, she started singing an old song, "zip-a-dee-doo-dah, zip-a-dee-ay, my oh my, what a wonderful day," she remembered from childhood. She said it helped considerably.

If you are in deep distress, and nothing seems to help, get help from a counselor. It can be a professional or just a friend who will allow you to cry on their shoulder. Remember that you went through a tremendous learning experience and expect to take something very positive about it. Remember to study your anger as if it is someone else feeling it. Do your best to avoid the triggers that set you off or thoroughly analyze them until they are no longer triggers. Study how you react to your anger and how you can change it. Substituting your pleasant parts for the awful details will help confuse your memory and can be very helpful in getting rid of the pain. Remember that the only good thing about anger is that it can spur you into action when you want to correct a grievance. As you improve your ability to manage it, you will be more and more in control of your life. It will also continue during your next phase of existence after leaving your earthly life.

Anger and any other painful emotion can harm your physical health and soul. Your soul feels everything you do just as strongly as your physical body does. It only makes sense to get rid of it any way you can. A much better way to prepare for our next stage of existence is to learn to feel joy, happy love, and success during this lifetime. And the time to work on love and happiness is right now. Picture yourself in a loving, warm, and happy relationship. Accept the fact, and it is a fact, that you are worthy of being loved deeply and dare to love many people during this lifetime. According to psychologist Fredrick Bartlett, "memories are organized within the historical and cultural frameworks of the individual, and the process of remembering involves the retrieval of information which has been unknowingly altered in order that it is compatible with preexisting knowledge." He says to change your feelings about the past, think back to the last time you felt angry with someone, and change various aspects of the scene in your mind, like the colors, the facial expressions of the person, and how you interact with them. Then gauge how they are feeling and what is causing them to act the way they do. Focus on the scene and ask them how they feel in your mind. Ask them in your mind if something caused them to feel this way. Ask them if they are taking out their self-hate on you or if someone abused them and if they are taking out their hurt on you. Then ask yourself how you feel and what made you think this way. Now replay the scene again and notice the changes in yourself and your thoughts about the situation. Are you still as angry? This process is straightforward to help you change memories and can be very effective. It can help you not only change your past; it can also help you recover from illness and turn problems into opportunities. Over time, with practice, you will feel a positive shift both mentally and physically.

Your thoughts and memories affect every cell in your body. Our thoughts and memories continually manifest our futures. You form your own set of morals you uphold from your memories. Remember, you are a spiritual entity who will exist forever, and it is better to experience love and joy than unhappiness and displeasure.

THOUGHTS

- All thought comes from your soul
- It is common to have false memories
- You can learn from your memories
- You can change and improve your memories
- Memories change for better or worse
- Memories influence your future
- Memories are spiritual self-communication
- Study your anger as if it is someone else's anger
- Your thoughts affect every cell in your body

CHAPTER 4
DISCOVERING MORALITY

AS A SPIRITUAL BEING, YOU ARE NOW WALKING AROUND in a physical body. When you began your time on earth in your new body, you slowly adjusted to it, even if you were here for a second or a thousandth time. Before you were born in this life, you spent time in your mother's womb. Your mother provided you with a comfortable and warm place where she delivered food to you to keep your body alive and growing. While in your warm, comfortable, and hopefully safe place, you could hear noises and voices from outside, but probably did not understand their significance to you.

Suddenly, one day, they transported you through a tunnel only to be deposited into a scene that was totally unfamiliar to you. You went through a profound and possibly overwhelming series of experiences as you moved from the womb to the outside world. The birth process is often a challenging and stressful experience. When you moved through the birth canal, you received tremendous stresses and pressure on your head and body. As soon as you reached daylight, immediately after coming out of the birth canal, they bombarded you with more new sensations. You saw shapes and lights, heard sounds, felt a new temperature, and touched new materials you have never felt before. (Or you had no memory of ever feeling them before.) They also bombarded your senses with new feelings and disorienting sensations. But you were intelligent enough to breathe to keep yourself alive. You shifted from receiving oxygen through a placenta to breathing air for your oxygen. This transition may have been easy, but you coughed as you pulled air into your lungs. You did it! You entered a new phase of your existence.

Once you no longer had a warm, safe, resting place and were out in the world, you had to regulate your own temperature. Initially, you may have felt cold, and someone may have placed you inside a warming device. And pretty quickly, you got hungry for the first time. You didn't have a tube fastened to you that kept you satisfied anymore. You got hungry, and you wanted food, and the only thing you knew to do was to yell that you wanted to be nourished and fed. You innately knew that if you made enough noise, it would get the attention of someone or something. You weren't worried about who or what would feed you. You just wanted food, and you wanted it immediately. And when that food came, usually through your mother's breast or some semblance of a breast, you innately knew to latch onto it and start sucking. You were barely out of the womb, and you already changed from depending completely on outside forces to keep your body viable to taking on the responsibility yourself. But you quickly formed a bond with the person who helped you get nourishment for your physical body. You understood they were the ones to depend on when you wanted to be comforted, receive affection, or be safe from anything you thought would endanger you.

You slept a lot, anywhere from 14 to 17 hours a day in these early moments of your physical life, but usually in short, irregular cycles. It was during this stage of growth you started your early childhood development. Over time, you focused your eyes and recognized familiar voices and faces. You also learned to deal with your senses of touch, taste, and smell. After you went through this stage, you were ready to learn how you, as a spiritual creature, would handle your time on earth. You learn simply by witnessing the activity which surrounds you both day and night.

By the time you started walking, you were developing the moral tone that you would carry with you throughout this life and into your journey to your next dimension after you leave Earth. That moral tone can be one of love or any tone between love and hate. Different people develop different moral tones. Some are born with a temper. For example, Sammy Fosdick was a rotten little child. He came out of the womb screaming the moment he was born. He brought a mean disposition with him when he started his human life. For the first few months of his life, if he wasn't sleeping or if someone wasn't holding him, he was crying and screaming. He would even cry when someone who he wasn't familiar with tried to pick him up and hold him.

The first day he was in kindergarten, he got into a fight with another boy, and his teacher called his parents in to have a conversation to determine how best to handle him. His parents were kind and loving people and couldn't understand where they had messed up in raising him. They admitted he was constantly getting into fights and causing havoc wherever he went. He seemed to have brought his ill temperament along with him when he was born. They had done their best to teach him the importance of kindness, honesty, and respect for others, but their attempts fell on deaf ears. Sammy did what he knew how to do, and that was always to be uncooperative and angry.

Sammy got into a lot of fistfights with the other children at school. He would win some of them, and he would lose some of them. In the fifth grade, he had a teacher called Mr. Simpson. Naturally, Sammy acted up on the first day of class. He started hitting the boy sitting next to him. Mr. Simpson saw what was going on and promptly walked over and comforted Sammy. He didn't say anything; he stood there looking at Sammy with a smile on his face. Sammy looked back at Mr. Simpson. They both stayed in place for about a minute, just looking at each other. Mr. Simpson kept smiling, and Sammy started fidgeting. No one had ever treated him like this before. He didn't know how to react. So, Sammy quieted down for the rest of the day. He was even quiet for several days before he started another fight in class. This time, Mr. Simpson walked over and again looked at Sammy with a smile on his face. Sammy immediately yelled at him and asked him what he wanted. He wanted to know why Mr. Simpson was looking at him like that. Mr. Simpson responded, still smiling, that he knew

Sammy could be an excellent student and help the other students, and he was curious to see when Sammy was going to be himself. This shut Sammy up, and he quieted down again.

After school that day, Sammy went to talk to Mr. Simpson and asked him why he didn't punish him. Mr. Simpson answered Sammy with a question, "Did you want me to?" Sammy paused and answered that he was supposed to punish him, to which Mr. Simpson smiled and said, "Oh?" The conversation went on for a while, with Mr. Simpson and Sammy becoming friends. After that day, they had many more conversations about Sammy's behavior. They would mainly speak about having positive moral values, being kind and having empathy for other people. Mr. Simpson explained to Sammy the importance of having a personal moral code and establishing limits on the behavior of others that you will accept. He also explained about the joy you receive when other people become happy because of your words or actions. And he explained how a happy life is not only more fun than being angry, but keeps you healthier and more intelligent.

The more Mr. Simpson talked to Sammy, the more Sammy understood it might be a good idea to change the way he treated people. For the first time in his life, he felt a smattering of guilt about the way he had behaved. Over the next several years, he changed his actions towards others. For example, when he was in the seventh grade, he noticed an elderly man struggling to carry two heavy bags to his car in a parking lot. Sammy quickly rushed to help him carry his bags to his car. The man thanked him deeply and offered him several dollars as a reward for his good deed, which Sammy refused to take. Sammy smiled and told the elderly gentleman it was just his way to get in a little exercise for himself. Then he thanked the man for allowing him to help.

Sammy's parents noticed he was changing, as he was nicer to them and was acting polite and with thoughtfulness. They felt overjoyed by Sammy's changes. His grades also went up in his school subjects. As the years passed, Sammy continued to treat people well, and he became popular at school, where his reputation for being thoughtful, kind, and nice had been growing. By the time he reached the 10th grade, they elected him to be president of his class. When the town he lived in suffered from tremendous damage caused by a tornado, Sammy organized a group of people to help repair homes and clear the debris from neighborhoods and streets. His efforts brought the members of the community closer together and the town emerged from the storm stronger than ever.

Sammy's soul entered its earthly existence filled with anger and hate. He was born bad, and he would continue his journey through eternity continually being bad, angry, and unhappy. But when he recognized there might be a better way for him to live, he changed his behavior, became a happier person, and helped other people improve their lives. He learned he could change, that it was never too late to change, and with the right attitude and determination, he could become a better person. As a result, he'll take the same morality with him throughout the rest of this life and into his next phase of existence.

Accepted morality differs in different parts of the world and changes as time changes. People believe Americans are now more compassionate than they were a century ago, but they also consider them more judgmental. It is easy to see that respect for authority has fallen in the past few years as has loyalty to, and pride in, our country. Other values, such as compassion, personal safety, and care for people less fortunate than others, have risen.

There is no universal standard as to what is moral and what is immoral. There are also different kinds of morality. Purity-based morality originates from ideas of sanctity and piety. When people violate purity-based standards, they often elicit reactions of repulsion and disgust. Authority-based morality prizes duty, deference, and social order and is slowly losing any power in the present time. Fairness-based morality is big at the present time. It stands in opposition to authority-based morality and judges right and wrong using values of equality, impartiality, and tolerance, and disdains bias and prejudice. Group-based morality esteems loyalty to family, community, or nation, and judges those who threaten or undermine them as immoral.

Harm-based morality values care, compassion, and safety. Its adherents view wrongness in terms of suffering, mistreatment, and cruelty.

People of different ages, genders, personalities, and political beliefs employ these moralities to different degrees. People on the political right are more likely to endorse the moralities of purity, authority, and ingroup loyalty, while those on the left rely more on the morality of harm and fairness. Women tend to endorse harm-based morality more than men. As cultures evolve and societies develop, people's ways of thinking about good and evil also go through changes. One narrative suggests our recent history is one of losing all morality. We have become more accepting of disruptive behavior, more rational, and irreligious. Another view claims we are becoming more moral. They claim our culture is increasingly censorious. We become offended and outraged over silliness, and the growing polarization of political debate reveals excesses of righteousness and self-righteousness.

We can see the decades since 1980 as a period when moral concerns experienced a revival. What has driven this revival is open to speculation. Some might see the election of conservative governments in the US, UK, and Australia at the start of this period as a pivotal change. That might explain the rise of typically conservative religious organizations. Others might point to the rise of social justice concerns—or "political correctness" to critics—as the basis for the upswing in harm-based morality. The surge of harmful language during early and mid-century wartime may point to the late-century rise being linked to the so called "culture wars." Certainly, the simultaneous rise in conservative (purity) and left-liberal (harm) moralities since that time is a recipe for moral conflict and polarization. In the last 50 years, we have also noticed a significant decrease in church attendance and an increase in spiritual exploration or nonmaterial energy. Our perception of what is right and wrong has changed from what it used to be, and if the trends continue, it will change in the future as well.

Just like a magnetic compass guides ships, a moral compass guides people. Also known as your conscience or your ethical principles, your moral compass is an innate set of values that guide your behavior and decisions. Your moral compass helps you distinguish between what's right and wrong. It plays a significant role in your life, and it guides the way you work, the way you respond when you're asked a question, the way you react to an event, or simply the way you go about your life. For example: Do you leave your campground clean or littered with trash? Do you lend your neighbor your lawn mower or claim you don't have one? Do you blame a mistake you made at work on your colleague or take responsibility for it?

Everything you experience in life affects the way you treat everything else in your life. Although you bring a certain morality with you when you are born, someone immediately exposes you to the behavior of other people. These people, whether they be parents, siblings, nurses, some kind of caregiver, or passing strangers, influence you. You immediately, subconsciously, if not consciously, pick up on the way other people act and you digest enough information to affect the way you will treat other people. When you go to school, you will have teachers and fellow students to learn more information that you will naturally add to your moral code.

The prime reason for the existence of many religions is to improve the moral behavior of their members. The religions profess that by following their guidelines, you will end up in a better place after you die. Everything that happens around you influences your moral principles; the political climate, the economic environment, the movies, television, and radio broadcasts all contribute to your morals. And they are open to change throughout your life. They change as you face new experiences, learn new information, cope with hardship, or even receive presents and goodies you appreciate.

As per the general morality of the present time, they consider you a good person if you show signs of living a good and purposeful life. Plain old honesty is considered highly respected and desired by everyone. They also consider the trait of humility desirable and worthy. That a person refrains from bragging about their accomplishments and isn't arrogant is good. It really does not take much to be considered as a person of high moral character. Simply showing respect for the thoughts and desires of other people will give you a seat at the table, like being a good friend and supportive of the people in your life. A big one is the habit of taking responsibility for your own actions, mistakes, and inadvertent faux pas. Things like being reliable, being kind to others and helping whenever you are called on, being considerate, being trustworthy, and compassionate are good moral principles in the present time. Also, being empathic is big.

You can feel spiritually strong when you have a well-defined moral code for yourself and clear boundaries for what you accept in your life, and you practice what you have defined for yourself. This will give you a strong sense of self-worth, integrity, and self-confidence. A well-developed moral code will help you find inner peace and happiness. It helps you think clearly in times of stress and promotes inner peace, even in times filled with stress. Your well-developed moral code will serve as a compass for you to create wonderful relationships with others because they will recognize you value their wants and needs. Wonderful relationships in return will bring you greater success in everything you attempt, because others will value your success and be more likely to help you attain your goals.

Develop Your Moral Code

No one is required to take time for themselves and define what they will tolerate from others and exactly the type of behavior they will expect from themselves. And only a small minority of people seriously study their own behavior. They bring themselves an opportunity to lead a better life than those who don't. Without your own personal moral code, you will often take actions based on your own immediate convenience without determining what is better for others, society, or you in particular. It can become easy to make decisions that will negatively impact those around you.

Criminals, psychopaths, and antisocial people often live with a perverted moral code. When spiritual people engage in shadow work or analyzing their inner child, which is simply looking deeply into themselves to find out what they are doing right or wrong, they are building their moral code. Your moral code encompasses your beliefs, principles, and values. It is helpful to reflect upon them and evaluate them from time to time, to ensure your code stays strong. You do this by reflecting on day-to-day situations. Ask yourself how you feel about what is happening in your life, both in the news and personally. You can even discuss your thoughts with others to see how they feel about them. While we can always consider how our actions will affect us, it's equally important to consider how they affect others. Putting yourself in someone else's shoes and seeing things from their perspective can help you understand how your actions might affect them. This can help you be more empathetic and guide your behavior toward them.

While your moral code guides you, it's important to follow through and stick with it. If you value punctuality, reliability, and trustworthiness, it's important to submit assignments on time and avoid making excuses for being late or messing up. The satisfaction you get by acting on your values is motivating and rewarding and will help strengthen your moral code and develop your spiritual strength. Your moral code will evolve over time. When you find something you once believed was mistaken or misguided, dare to correct yourself. Admit your mistakes, apologize to people you've hurt, and learn from every situation. Even if you were mistaken before, correcting yourself can help you strengthen your moral code and help you feel at peace with yourself. Being stubborn and refusing to accept that you might have been wrong can be as harmful to your mental well-being as it is to others'.

As we go through life, a continuous stream of events will come into our lives that challenge us to examine our beliefs and how we need to react to the actions and words of others. You may go months or even years without facing a circumstance that will challenge you, but you could have many challenges within a single day. You should always stay alert to the possibility of encountering an opportunity that offers you spiritual growth or challenges you. Allow yourself to be curious about any unfamiliar situation or even offers that appear to be too good to be true. Keep your trait of curiosity alive and active.

THOUGHTS

- You were born with innate knowledge
- You brought a moral code with you when you were born
- You continue to develop your moral code while living on Earth
- Even the worst people can change
- Accepted moral codes change over time
- Accepted morals may differ in different parts of the world
- Every human has at least a semblance of a moral code
- Evaluate yourself to improve your moral code
- Stick to your own well-thought-out moral code

CHAPTER 5
THE CURIOSITY FACTOR

PEOPLE ON THE SPIRITUAL PATH STUDY HOW TO REACH states of love, joy, harmony, and calm emotions. They want to train for the time when they can exist in a constant state of Nirvana, and they believe the time to work toward their goal is right now. They want to attune their body, mind, and soul to be in tune with the vibratory energy of the Universe. It is not a simple path to follow because the idea of a person being in tune with the Universe instead of doing what everyone else is doing is scary. Spiritual people differ from religious people in how they view their relationship with God. Many religious people believe there is a separation between God and us. In fact, in many religions the church leaders, whether minister, priest, or elder, act as the interpreter of God's word for their adherents. Spiritual people tend to feel they are composed of the same material as God. Religious people pray to God, asking Him for help, guidance, or to provide whatever they want. They also pray to thank God for the things they receive. Spiritual people are more inclined to ask the Universe to cooperate with them. They manifest, affirm, or visualize what they want. They want to be in harmony with the Universe or what some call the Source.

John E. had spiritual parents, and he followed in their footsteps. While growing up, he meditated, visualized, and practiced most of the things spiritual people do. He did well in school and got a good job after college graduation. Soon after graduation, he married his one and only wife and started a family. He started his own business within 10 years and is now a successful businessperson. He is a typical spiritual person.

Spiritual people are naturally inclined to develop harmony with other people. While existing on Earth, spiritual people take care of their essential needs to allow them to feel joy and to thrive. They see their time on Earth as an opportunity to prepare for the next dimension in which they will exist. That is what John did, and it worked. John understood that everything he ever did would deal with a human need while meeting a spiritual need. John was fortunate; he never seemed to go through the difficulties many people experience before they become spiritual. He understood if people work at a job and earn money, they can support their basic needs of food, shelter, and clothing. They can probably also provide a means of transportation for themselves. Their soul is also learning to cooperate with others to manage their needs.

Spiritual people want to have a direction in their lives, and they claim the responsibility to discover and follow it. They want to feel confident they can meet their basic needs for food, shelter, and clothing. They also work to achieve control of their emotions in order to enjoy life. It is essential for most spiritual people to know the sun will rise every day and to have the work that they want. Most people desire comfort and certainty in at least one form or fashion. When they don't have their basic needs met, it can cause anxiety, fear, and hunger.

Spiritual people are curious about the world unless the curiosity trait got smothered in their childhood. Even if it was beaten out of them when they were young, it will probably bloom again in their adult years. They have an ingrained need to explore variety in their lives. They like an adventure to mix things up from time to time. Having a safe place to spend time is nice, but they always want to experience something new and different. They don't know why, but it is ingrained in their spiritual fiber. For example, they enjoy knowing they have a pleasant home in which to live. However, they enjoy taking off on vacation to explore unknown places once in a while. While they may deny they like variety, they love it. It's important to them to enjoy new experiences, continuously learn, and find harmony with others and within themselves.

They also have a deep-seated need to feel significant and to be helpful to others. Maybe it is in their work, marriage, or desire to influence others spiritually and logically. If so, there's absolutely nothing wrong with that. We all do. We all want life to have meaning and significance. When others benefit through their actions, spiritual people feel the improvement emotionally. It makes them feel good and encourages them to look for others to help. Their helping others is not selfish. They don't do it to receive accolades or glory. They do it because it makes them feel good. They don't even consider how their goodness helps strengthen their own spiritual muscle. It is a powerful way to help oneself prepare for a loving, joyous future.

Even spiritual introverts, who appreciate their alone time and associate with fewer people than your average extrovert or ambivert, occasionally need to connect with others. All spiritual people want to develop loving relationships where everyone supports the activities and ideas of each other. They appreciate the feeling of being loved and respected by others. They have a deep desire for honest and loving relationships. It is often difficult for them to overcome the hurt, fear, and anger directed at them by others.

One of the most important reasons for spirits to spend time on Earth is to expand their understanding of the various situations they will meet throughout eternity. They want to experience difficulties along with times of harmony to learn to improve and keep a joyful equilibrium. They need to expand and grow their perspective on reality. Children act curious because it is natural for spiritual energy to seek new experiences. They want to expand and grow mentally, emotionally, physically, spiritually, and in any other way. Often, spiritual people don't think they are growing, but they are growing anyway.

With every problem they meet, they have a chance to learn what works or what doesn't work. When they realize whether or not they are successful, it is an opportunity to increase their understanding of how the Universe works. It becomes an understood opportunity for them. Spiritual people also usually want to contribute value to humanity in some way. Many of them take the saying too seriously, "It is better to give than receive." Parents teach them this when they are young. When they reach maturity, many of them understand that receiving is also good. They realize just as they receive joy when giving something worthwhile to others, others receive satisfaction when people give presents to them. It works both ways. It can be just as good to receive as it is to give once you understand gratitude.

Our time on Earth is a terrific opportunity to gain experience in living in harmony with the people we associate with and the Universe. According to the *Cambridge English Dictionary*, harmony is a situation in which people are peaceful and agree with each other, or in which different things seem right or suitable together. Life isn't always harmonious, but when it is, it is usually very pleasurable. You can experience harmony when you listen to music, watch a dance group, or share in almost any way with others. Harmonious relationships where you get along with other people can be gratifying.

Our modern way of living can exasperate anyone, like when you call on your cell phone to speak with someone you want to work on your house, make a doctor's appointment, or even go out to dinner. First, you dial the number, and when a voice answers, you get a choice of five or six numbers to punch in to get more information. Then, when you get transferred, you get even more options to choose from, and this time you realize you made the wrong choice. No, you can't just change it. You have to hang up and start all over again. Your once-friendly feeling of harmony and bliss suddenly turns to flaming rage. You take a deep breath and make your call once more. Finally, after another five minutes of being transferred through different options, you reach your party, and everything is perfectly harmonious between you and the person you are talking with. That is the story of life. We have pleasurable experiences and not-so-good experiences.

Life is an ongoing journey to develop harmony in our lives in such a way that allows us to avoid or overcome horrible experiences and continue to experience harmonious times without them becoming monotonous or boring. The ideal life of a spirit while on Earth is to wake up every morning feeling happy, jubilant, and excited. Developing this ability to wake up happy and well-adjusted every morning takes wisdom and practice. People often make the mistake of judging intelligence over wisdom. You can be the most intelligent or smartest person in the world, but if you can't make wise decisions, you might be less well off than the village idiot.

Almost any government agency run by politicians is an excellent example of wisdom being better than intelligence. Politicians get chosen because they cheat or are smart enough to determine how to win without cheating. Either way, it takes a certain amount of brain power. They get elected, and the next thing you know, they are passing laws that impede the rights of the members of their community. They overspend their budgets and suddenly become wealthy by doing nothing except having a few rich friends who profit from the laws they pass. When spiritual people focus on developing the trait of wisdom, which is the ability to make excellent decisions, they make tremendous spiritual growth. The proper spiritual life is not one of hiding away in a monastery and praying every day for years and years. It is one of experiencing the highs and lows of different activities. Spiritual people are like everyone else, except they realize that their soul is the principle motivating factor in their life.

The souls that spend time on Earth vibrate at speeds ranging from very high to extremely low. There are more and more souls vibrating at high levels and fewer and fewer souls vibrating at lower levels than there were in the past. The good spirits are gradually overtaking the evil spirits. When humanity first populated the Earth, people didn't consider the feelings, wants, or needs of others. It was a game of taking what you could get and not worrying about anybody else.

When they slowly developed the idea there was a God or a bunch of gods who had power over them, they changed their behavior. Certain members of those societies spoke out and claimed that God would punish the bad guys. Most people who spoke out promptly got killed for speaking with audacity. Jesus Christ is a prime example. The evil spirits are still with us but slowly losing their power to commit evil deeds as they learn the power of love, joy, and harmony.

Different varieties of these cruel, oppressive souls work for governments throughout the world. They either reach their positions of authority through inheritance from their parents, take it forcefully, or through elections, many of which they or their sponsors control the results. Good spirits developed the United States of America by using force to overthrow a robust regime, just as other countries did in the past. Unlike earlier powers, the kind and wise souls who chartered the United States produced a document giving freedom to its citizens. The first two amendments gave the people freedom of speech and the power to defend themselves. They felt lucky to succeed but doubted that the government would last longer than 50 years. The government still exists but is going through a power struggle to figure out which type of spiritual people will control it. If the good spirits win, it will be an example for the rest of the world and begin another slow but powerful movement for freedom for all souls on Earth. There is a possibility that a country led by one or more evil spirits will start exploding nuclear bombs all over the planet and cause enough destruction to set back its evolution into a world of love, harmony, and joy for at least a thousand years. No matter what happens in the next few years, the change toward love, joy, and peace will continue its predestined path to fulfillment.

Each human being, who is also a tiny part of this massive spiritual entity called Source, God, or Universe, plays an essential role in this spiritual journey to Nirvana. Meanness, ugliness, and nastiness spreads throughout the Universe through contagion, like love, joy, and harmony. No human is intrinsically bad or good, and neither is their soul. They pick up these energies from people they associate with or sometimes out of the clear air. Kindhearted, gentle, and loving people occasionally indulge themselves as an aggressively mean essence of spiritual energy. They feel hate, anger, or whatever they have seen previously. They revert to acting angry themselves. They must learn to calm themselves and speak with love and joy. When another empathetic soul foams at the mouth or generates vicious clouds of anger, the truly spiritual person must learn to withstand it and continue to radiate with a demeanor of love, joy, and harmony. Once a person does this, they will become like the Buddha, Jesus, and other well-known figures from the past. They were spiritual people, and it makes sense that spiritual people should emulate other spiritual people.

Spiritual people tend to relax and treat others with respect and joy. The wiser ones do their best to develop harmony in their every relationship. This attitude has contributed to the slow but powerful change in man's behavior during the past 400,000 years. There are millions of spiritual people traversing the Earth right now. As more and more people recognize they are spiritual beings, they will continue to accept the natural spiritual behaviors which will bring worldwide peace, harmony, love, and joy.

Spiritual energy naturally wants acceptance and harmony in everything it does. The acts of meditation, grounding, journaling, and developing the traits of gratitude and inner love will continue to improve the entire planet's atmosphere. When a spiritual person experiences harmony in their spiritual and physical essence, it can feel exhilarating. Peace comes about when you are in tune with the people you currently associate with. Examples include when you dance with a partner you love and sync your steps with each other. It feels good. Another example happens when you are on a sports team and your team is winning. It also feels good. The goal of most spirits is to develop a continual feeling for the various states of harmony, love, joy, wisdom, honesty, and good physical health. The emotions must vary in their degree of expression because without variance, they will become boring. Most spiritual people come to Earth lacking one or more of these properties, and their time on Earth gives them the time to learn about them and improve them.

Once fully developed and often only barely developed, spiritual people are the shining stars or powerful energy forces that instigate change in others. As said earlier, spiritual energy is contagious. It not only attracts similar power, but it also influences all energy around it. It is often slow-acting because negative energy is infectious and slightly weaker than positive energy. The slow speed of this contagion is the primary reason it has taken thousands of years to grow from the fearful and hostile stages of early humankind to the semi-peaceful state we live in today. Every second of every minute you spend in a relationship with another person, you influence each other. There is rarely an immediate change in either person's positive or negative attitudes. It often takes thousands of moments together to effect minor changes. Spiritual energy, although contagious, has little power. You can help the World become a better place simply by daring to be your best self. You will help when you tell others you are spiritual and want to be happy, loving, harmonious, and wise. They may or may not appreciate it, but they will often cooperate with you.

The very act of telling another person how to treat you helps to strengthen your spiritual essence. It is like working out physically in a gym. The more you do it, the stronger you get. If you aren't already doing it, the time to start is right now. You can visualize yourself doing it, manifest it, journal for it, and affirm it as practice. See yourself doing it in every type of situation. Even when people react to you negatively, you need to continue to express your joy in a calm, relaxed manner. After all, you are practicing having a well-developed future of powerful happiness. Practice living as your vision of the perfect you every day, and you will significantly advance toward spiritual perfection in this lifetime. You will also influence others in ways that will help them grow. It will not be overnight, but the creation of a worldly paradise will advance faster than ever.

When humanity first climbed out of the sea, it consisted of tiny creatures that could barely crawl. It took thousands of years to grow large enough to walk on two legs. Then it took another significant amount of time to grow vocal cords and communicate with each other by grunting and making sounds. It took even longer to learn how to communicate with words than grunts, emotions, and gestures. Our spiritual energy is changing and evolving every second of our lives.

In sports, athletes break records every year. Someone runs faster or jumps higher than anyone ever has before. Each generation of children grows bigger and stronger than their parents' generation. In the future, they may grow smaller and weaker, but there will be changes in their body makeup. As spiritual creatures, we humans have the fantastic opportunity to gain experience and adjust to the changes we will experience throughout eternity. We have no provable information about where our next period of existence will be.

Spiritually, you are liable to land anywhere. The Universe is composed of spiritual energy that can become any form it chooses. Plants grow better when treated with love. The roots of trees grow toward other trees close to them. Plants and trees don't communicate the same way humans do, but it appears they speak to each other. Also, trees live much longer than humans and adjust to their long lives. Many people will reject the idea, but with all the scientific discoveries about the energies of the Universe, it appears the Universe is one humongous brain, and each of us is a tiny part of it.

It doesn't matter if you believe the Universe is a singular spiritual creature or if you are an atheist or believe we are distinctly different creatures living for a few years and then dropping dead. Most people would like to spend this life enjoying varied feelings of love, joy, appreciation, respect, and experiencing beautiful relationships with other people. Every moment can be a learning experience. It starts with the desire to be happy, to feel good about oneself, and to experience success in worldly endeavors. Once you have the passion, you must take action to achieve your goals. Most people have never thought about developing plans for themselves because no one told them it would be a good idea. Back in the 1950s, a book by Napoleon Hill called *Think and Grow Rich* inspired millions of people to do that.

They read the book and made big plans for themself that they did not accomplish. Nevertheless, the book was so exciting to them they kept trying and soon started having success. Our job while we live on Earth is to learn about love, joy, and harmony and to achieve a little wisdom. As spiritual creatures, we are here to learn to exist in varying degrees of harmony and happiness. Our inbred curiosity drives us into endeavors which help us. Having harmony in our lives is a priority.

THOUGHTS

- The spiritual path is not always easy
- Spiritual Energy is the base energy of the Universe
- Spiritual people are curious people
- It is as good to receive as to give
- Spiritual living invites both good and bad experiences
- Good spiritual energy is slowly defeating bad energy
- Spiritual energy is contagious
- You improve the World by being your best self

CHAPTER 6
THE SEARCH FOR HARMONY

IT IS EASY TO UNDERSTAND THAT HUMANS ARE SPIRITUAL beings wearing physical bodies during their time on Earth. It is a little harder to realize that our spiritual selves, our souls, control our every thought, emotion, and movement. Understanding that our souls are inherently curious may be a little more challenging. We know there is a law of change, meaning that change is inherent in all energy forms and the energy of which we are composed is always seeking something new. This seeking is the basis for the intrinsic curiosity everyone has. When you look back at the history of humankind, it is easy to notice the advancements in every aspect of living we have made over the years. We started as small people, and now we are reasonably tall and growing taller and more robust every few decades. We used to die after only a few years, and now the average life expectancy is over 70 years.

In the beginning, we traveled on foot and didn't wear clothes. Now we travel in cars, planes, boats, and rocket ships. One of the most beautiful aspects of our eternal existence is that we experience new realities in every incarnation and dimension in which we exist. They say, "Where your attention goes, your energy flows." The curiosity factor is one aspect of our makeup that can make our journey through eternity enjoyable. As human beings, we constantly question and explore our surroundings. While existing on Earth, spiritual people want to take care of their essential needs that allow them to enjoy life and thrive. They see their time on Earth as an opportunity to prepare for the next dimension in which they will exist. They usually understand that everything they ever do will deal with a human need and meet a spiritual need. If they work at a job to earn money, they will support their basic needs. They can probably also provide a means of transportation for themselves. Some people don't need money for food, shelter, and clothing because they have great wealth, but they still have to put out the effort to attain fresh supplies and keep their wealth.

Spiritual people want honest, loving relationships in their lives. They also want to achieve control of their emotions, which will enable them to enjoy life. Most people desire comfort, certainty, and to grow spiritually in this life. Our life on Earth is a beautiful time to learn how to manufacture our feelings of love, joy, and harmony.

Another important reason for spirits to spend time on Earth is to expand their understanding of the various situations they will encounter throughout eternity. They will experience a series of difficulties on and off throughout their lives to learn to improve and maintain their joyful equilibrium. They need to expand and grow their perspective on reality. Children are curious because it is only natural for them to be interested in new things. They want to expand and grow mentally, emotionally, physically, spiritually, and in almost every other way. Often, spiritual people don't think they are growing, but they are likely growing spiritually anyway. With every problem they encounter, they have a chance to learn what works or what doesn't work. When they realize that whether or not they are successful, it is an opportunity to increase their understanding of how the Universe operates; it becomes an understood opportunity for them. They want to grow and excel in various areas of life.

Spiritual people typically want to produce harmony, happiness, and love in everything they experience. They want harmony with their closest friends, family, business life, and other relationships, including their mental, physical, and spiritual health. They also endeavor to develop harmony with those who have different thoughts and ideas than they do. They want to create the wisdom to collaborate with people of different persuasions than themselves. In other words, they endeavor to develop insight into their life.

Developing harmony in any facet of life can be challenging work. But when you think about it for a little while, you realize you put in just about the same effort, and maybe a little more effort, into producing disharmony in your life. Spiritual people don't have commandments to which they have to abide. Still, they have truisms or spiritual guidelines, and one of them says there is no such thing as a perfect relationship. They all take effort. There are challenges in most relationships because all parties experience different obstacles to handle in their own lives. As we learn to manage our blocks, triggers, and times of trauma, we also learn ways to build harmony with others. We improve in ways that will help us spiritually.

Once you accept this, you will save energy and gain strength and vitality, making you a better person. My friend Ernie gets along with everyone. He always smiles and appears happy. I asked him his secret, and he told me he treats people how he wants them to treat him. He also told me he maintains his boundaries. If you know Ernie, he will treat you respectfully and kindly. He is the type of person you want for a best friend. His soul lives in harmony. He has learned his lessons well, which he will carry with him for years.

You are the one person who decides whether or not you will be happy at any given time. Your thoughts trigger your emotions, and you feel whatever the message is that your body receives from your thoughts. Your ideas come from your soul. You think unhappy thoughts, and you will be sad. Happy thoughts will make you feel satisfied. Sometimes, society considers it proper for you to be low, like when a relative dies or becomes deathly ill. But when you allow yourself to sink to unhappiness over a hurtful or sad situation, you waste time when you could think up ways to help the situation. You can even think of how to improve the case, or even react positively if worse slides down to worst. Of course, it is only natural to mourn because of the death of a loved one, but mourning can interfere with one's ability to make wise decisions. One lesson we can learn while we spend time on Earth is how to deal with horrific circumstances in a calm and intelligent manner. Have you ever thought about being happy for someone who died because they have embarked on a new adventure? You are a spiritual being and pass the time however you want to while you exist on Earth. The worst events, like the best ones, will not be with you a hundred years from now. You handle your health, attitude, point-of-view, and reactions to everything you experience during this lifetime. You can turn your anger into happiness, understanding, empathy, sympathy, love, or anything else you want. Other people are also just acting out their feelings. Very few people pause long enough to think about how they can make the best of any situation. It is easier when you are around other loving, joyful people, but you can do it alone. You can be the person who uplifts others when you focus on uplifting thoughts, success, and positive change.

What you experience every second of your life is real and a rehearsal for your future. You are practicing today's reality for how you will experience a similar truth in the future. People often develop a bucket list for everything they want to do when they retire. Then, when they reach retirement age, they are too tired, too broke, or not healthy enough to follow through on their bucket list. As said earlier, live in the now and not just for tomorrow or next year. You can enjoy every moment of your life, feel love all the time, and flat-out enjoy life.

Spiritual people need to invest in their health while still living. You might say, "A healthy body equals a healthy soul." Although your body is just the uniform you wear while you live, it constantly affects your soul. Your body is the structure your soul uses during your time on Earth. If it isn't working correctly, it makes it more difficult for your soul to operate. Exercise is also essential because it helps you stay healthy. When you exercise, your body releases endorphins which interact with receptors in your brain. This reduces your feelings of pain and triggers positive and energizing feelings and an optimistic outlook on life. Being a couch potato or dependent on medicine will not give you the energy that a regimen of exercise will. Myriads of people use drugs to help them become more in tune with their spiritual selves. Using drugs to help you become in tune with your spirituality is a fruitless exercise. It is a valid excuse for using drugs to relax, though. You connect with your spiritual self, whatever you believe. Your thoughts come from your soul. Your soul uses your brain as the software uses a computer, and you use your body to put your ideas into action. An expression goes, "Use it or lose it." This expression flatly means that if you don't use your body, you will not have it to use anymore. Your body is a necessary appendage for you to use to carry out your mission during your stay on earth.

When your body and soul are healthy, your ability to develop harmonious relationships is at its peak. Good relationships help build a good, happier, and healthier life. It is a win-win situation. Harvard University did a 75-year study of adult life that showed good relationships keep people happier and healthier. This study states that having at least one person with whom you can be close makes sense. It did not say that money, high achievement, or fame would make you happy and healthy. We often hear about how unhappy famous people are. Our number of friends has nothing to do with our health and happiness. The media are happy to publicize famous people's arguments, divorces, and disasters. But they are no more happy or unhappy than anyone else.

The lessons about our positive relationships with our family and friends are good for us. Poor relationships are not beneficial for us. Loneliness is terrible for us. Wealthy and famous people with supposedly many friends can be very lonely. They may know many people, but have no one in which to confide. Good relationships don't just protect our bodies. They protect our brains and our souls. We are more alert when communicating with people we respect or accept as close to us. It is also easier to feel love for them and feel gratitude for their friendship. Every spiritual person subconsciously needs to develop love, gratitude, harmony, and cooperative traits. You can do this. Society often tries to interfere with the progress of spiritual people with their rules and regulations, but love and gratitude will eventually win out.

It seems reasonable that most people want to feel happiness or joy throughout eternity. Unhappiness does not have much appeal to any good person, but many people seem to spend most of their lives being unhappy with their circumstances. They complain about things you do and speak about. They complain about things that happen to them. They say it is never their fault, but the world never treats them right. They want to go to heaven, where they will spend their time happily adoring God. It sounds like magic and, if true, will be magic. The law of change and vibration ensures that our souls constantly evolve emotionally. We develop spiritual power as we learn to keep our emotions moving in a high range of happiness and love. If our souls were not constantly changing, our state of joy would become very uncomfortable and dull. We should strive to know how to generate varied levels of love, joy, and harmony for eternity.

Some people don't even seem to know what it is like to feel love, joy, and harmony. To do this, it takes deep self-examination which is shadow work and honestly accepting your own self-worth. You need to know the true meanings of the words, know what they feel like and have the courage to display them. That is what this life is all about. We are on a journey to learn about spiritual love, happiness, and gratitude.

THOUGHTS

- We come from the material of God or the Universe
- Spiritual people want to cooperate with their God
- This Earth life is a preparation for future lives
- Spiritual people look for harmony in their lives
- Spiritual people need variety in life
- It is essential to take care of your basic needs
- Spiritual people desire to contribute value to society
- A healthy body is helpful to the soul

CHAPTER 7
SPIRITUAL LOVE, HAPPINESS, AND GRATITUDE

OUR EMOTIONS CONTINUALLY CHANGE, ALTHOUGH WE all have a default emotion we spend most of our time experiencing. Your feelings tell you exactly how your soul feels. People rarely think about improving the quality of their feelings, but it is a worthwhile task. There are several ways you can improve them.

Get in the habit of being thankful. Try keeping a journal of activities for which you are grateful. Research shows that people who record their daily blessings are optimistic about their lives, have a happy framework about life, and tend to be healthy. Start by spending a short time journaling daily. Make it fun. Use a bulletin board for notes, or even the front of your refrigerator. Attach small reminders of things that make you feel grateful, such as a kind note from a friend or even a picture of anything for which you feel thankful.

Make it a point to celebrate the minor victories in your life. Say it is a beautiful day outside. The weather is perfect, the sun is shining, and you feel fine. Celebrate it by going for a walk or just going out and breathing the air. Say you know someone who gets a raise or masters a new skill. Give them a small present or send them a congratulatory note. Any little thing will do. They will appreciate your thoughtfulness, and you will feel good about doing it. By doing little things, like giving a small present or sending a congratulatory note, you can build up your habit of delighting others.

Another simple way to develop the gratitude habit is to send a thank you note, complimentary letter, or email to someone every day. Make this a habit and compliment a different person each day. Doing this compels you to think about people you know. They appreciate it, and it will force you to focus on something good about other people. You will see the power of this act when your relationships with other people improve, and your social life becomes more rewarding. When you are in the middle of an exciting or fantastic event, savor it. Then tell your friends about it and remember your thoughts and emotions. The idea is to experience the good feelings repeatedly until they become your normal state of awareness. Recognize that right now is always a chance to experience love, harmony, and joy. Realize you can generate this happy feeling whenever you want and show yourself you are naturally optimistic. The average person spends much of their time expressing the wrong kinds of thoughts. They spend much of their time focusing on how they will fail in their latest endeavor rather than on how they will succeed and what a great feeling they will have when they succeed.

Take a few minutes and ask yourself what is important to you. It will help if you have a clear picture of what it is, whether you want to lead a happy life, or you want to keep working until you reach old age. Whatever it is, focus on bringing it into your life to help you experience ecstasy. You are spiritual or subtle energy, and you will always be energy. As a being composed of spiritual energy, you are eternal and ever-changing.

The memories will change, the information will continually change, and the emotions will change. Still, you can use your memory to keep the current information you know and feel in your soul at a high level of happiness. Keep your focus on experiencing gratitude for about six weeks because it takes about that long for new habits to form. Learn to appreciate all the minor positive events that enter your life. The ideal scenario would be to wake up in the morning feeling gratitude and go to sleep feeling gratitude.

When you wake up in the morning with a positive mindset, you can approach the day with positive expectations that everything will be happy, successful, and prosperous for the rest of the day. Throughout the day, you will have your typical difficulties and good times. But if you keep track, you may find there are more ups than downs. When evening comes, review the things that went well for you. Think about the good things that happened to you during the day. Focus on anything that makes you feel better. Allow the good feelings to spread through your body and compliment yourself for surviving anything that didn't go well. Suppose you have difficulty falling asleep. In that case, it may be because you think about a problem you had that day or a challenge you believe you will have the next day instead of something that makes you feel good. Change your focus to find anything you can feel good about. Changing your negative thoughts to positive ones is a robust and reliable way to change them. Being thankful for what you have signals the Universe, and in return, the Universe sends you more. Every thought sends a message to the Universe about how you expect to feel. The Universe, in return, does its best to accommodate your wishes.

Remember things you do well, appreciate that you can do them, and then do them often. If you have a pet, it probably loves you and trusts you. Notice how happy it is when you pay attention to it. It is a spiritual creature like you. You can show other people love, appreciation, and loyalty, just like your pet shows you. (But you really don't need to bother wagging your tail.)

Be thankful while contemplating the good that has happened to you. Everyone you have ever known has contributed to helping you become the person you are today. Some of them have treated you with love and kindness. A few people have possibly criticized you. Be thankful for those who treated you well because they taught you how to treat others and helped you feel good about yourself. Be grateful to the ones who criticized you as well. They pointed out something for you to improve and gave you an opportunity to enhance your ability to chill out when things weren't going well.

There are all kinds of things for which you can be grateful. You live in an environment where you can learn new ways to create happiness. Being spiritual, you undoubtedly have a good heart and enjoy seeing others doing well. You have food to eat and a roof over your head. You likely have clean water and someone in your family or friends who cares for you. You also have clothes to wear. And you can smile. Remember to think about the things you are grateful for every day. And remember, you can improve your ability to experience gratitude by comparing how you would be without the gifts, help, and friendship of others.

Practice Self-Love

As spiritual beings, we are composed of memory, information, and emotion that is always working with our soul. Everything we ever do involves our soul. Emotions are one way our souls present information to our bodies. Learn what your feelings are telling you, especially those that cause you pain, so you can take loving action when responding to them. Ask yourself what you are thinking or doing that causes your painful feelings of guilt, shame, anxiety, anger, loneliness, emptiness, or whatever. Allow the answer to come from your spiritual essence, soul, and feelings. When you understand what is causing these thoughts and feelings, ask yourself how to change your position from being a victim of your emotions to being relaxed and in control. Open your heart to receiving messages you can feel good about, which will help you love yourself. The key is to be open to the possibility you can love yourself and it is right for you to do so. If someone taught you that self-love is a sin, this might not be easy, but it becomes easier and easier as you keep doing it.

It is implausible that people who genuinely love themselves do anything to harm others. It is not suitable for them to hurt people who will dislike them and possibly damage them in response. The experience of feeling love for others and the ability to receive and accept the love of others is a primary goal for people who want to enter their afterlife in good standing.

Love for yourself and others are both beautiful feelings, and nothing is better when you can incorporate them with happiness. When you can accomplish this while still living, you are very fortunate. A relationship with another person is a normal and natural part of living. We, as humans, form bonds with each other. When someone lacks the ability to develop a healthy bond with another person, it can cause problems like depression, loneliness, anxiety, addiction, and many other unsavory conditions.

Most of what we know about connecting with others comes from how we interacted with our immediate family as we grew up. Were our parents attentive to us, unpredictable, or even dismissive? Were our parents huggers? Did they hug each other and us a lot? Did they spend a lot of time with us? Or did they mostly ignore us? These things affect the way we act toward others when we reach adulthood. Also, how our friends and siblings behave towards us affects how we treat others as adults.

In today's world, a couple gets together, and they call it love. They meet several times and then become a couple, not because of any love, but because they have no one else to love. So, they do their best. Often, an empath will end up with a narcissist. Or two lonely people who have no one else get together and stay lonely together while never really getting to know each other. Although society seems to dictate that people can only love one person at a time, it is healthy to love many people. When you can truly love people, you will always want what is best for others and appreciate them. You do not need to love only one person. The more people you can love, the better it is for you. And people you love will appreciate it when you tell them you love them. You do not have to have a romantic relationship with them; you simply need to have the pleasure of loving them.

People say that narcissistic people love themselves. But when narcissistic people form relationships, they always end up causing hurt, even though they are supposed to benefit from these relationships.

It is difficult to believe they ever really gain anything except the eventual loss of respect from the people they abuse. It may be self-hate, though, as one can only love another as one loves oneself. Love should never be exhausting or leave you feeling stressed out or less than you deserve. Love is supposed to be free of the everyday stresses of life. It doesn't leave you feeling drained or unappreciated. Love is a healer, a protector, and a friend. It will bring out the best in you, heal you, and strengthen you spiritually.

There are many other types of love depending on who defines them. Spiritually, it is essential to feel a love that embraces gratitude, harmony, and joy. It is also good to have a strong sense of love for yourself because you cannot love another person any more than you can love yourself. People will argue with that statement, but they are wrong. Dr. Deb Hirschhorn, a marriage and family therapist, said, "If you think you love someone else more than yourself, it's not love in the first place. You didn't love them that much, and you surely didn't love yourself that much either." She further explained, "It's neediness. Self-love is knowing you are worth loving and treating yourself as if you are someone you love. It knows you are worthwhile."[3] Self-love is a difficult step in the right direction for many people.

As more and more spiritual people learn to love themselves, they will contribute more and more to the future paradise on Earth. There are a few steps to take in learning to love yourself. The first thing to do is learn to take responsibility for your feelings. Many people blame their bad feelings on others or situations they don't like. They are your feelings, and you are the one who is responsible for them and can be in control of them. No one else can do these things. Recognize your feelings and accept them. Refuse to run away from them by using alcohol, drugs, sweets, judging yourself, blaming them on others, or using other types of destructive behaviors. They are your feelings, and their purpose is to communicate with you. Your soul communicates

---

3   Deb Hirschhorn, "Can You Love Someone Else More Than Yourself?," Drdeb.com, accessed February 7, 2024, https://drdeb.com/can-you-love-someone-else-more-than-yourself/.

with you through your feelings. It is your responsibility to listen to them and keep them in a positive state.

Embrace Appreciation, Tolerance, and Spiritual Love

By the time we reach adulthood, very few of us are naturally loving, open, cheerful, optimistic, and easily approachable. We have developed many behaviors we learned from our families and friends. But they aren't always helpful in creating a fulfilling life. As adults, we pair up with another human being and say we love that other person. Still, very few of us know what spiritual love is. We may have read many definitions of love. But the definitions only describe the behaviors of how we love in different ways. Spiritual love, pure love, beneficial love, super love, or whatever you want to call it, should be unique. It should never impede the melding of spiritual togetherness. Instead, it should have beautiful qualities to help you maintain a happy and healthy life. Without trust, there is the possibility of doubt in what the other person says, thinks, or does. When you feel spiritual love for someone, you trust them completely. Love is all good. There is nothing negative about it. Appreciation is a powerful component of spiritual love. You may even appreciate a smile or a kind word from someone you love. In fact, without the ability to enjoy the actions of others, it is difficult to feel any love at all. The ability to feel appreciation is a significant component of spiritual love.

Another component of spiritual love is tolerance. Give your loved ones the freedom to act as they please without getting upset. You aren't attached to the other person so tightly that you need to control them. There is mutual respect. Yes, when you love someone, there will still be differences of opinion and occasional arguments. If there are still differences of view, the partners respect and accept them, and the arguments end quickly. When you have boundaries, and your loved one will appreciate them just as you will respect their boundaries.

To develop an exemplary case of true spiritual love, you need to be a mature adult. When you achieve this ability, you become powerful spiritually. You will carry this same ability when you transcend to your next destination. Love is easy to grow into, but people make it hard because they focus on the actions and words of other people. They are lied to, cheated, abused, manipulated, and taught to behave by people who know nothing and care very little about love. Today's spiritual people are concerned with these kinds of things. As they practice loving as it should be done, and expect others to treat them properly, spiritual love will spread. It is already spreading.

Earth is a marvelous place to learn and practice spiritual love. Our physical parts respond to information directed to them from our souls, and we react with more force and strength to our physical components than to our spiritual aspects. That extra strength has a better chance of impressing our souls when we act like animals and human beings than in our spiritual state. The difference is like being hit with a hammer rather than a feather. You can treat the earth like a vacation place, a prison, a torture chamber, or a wonderful place filled with adventure and romance. Because we have free will, we can make of our stay here whatever we want.

The world's population continues to grow year after year. Every type of living creature breeds more and more creatures of the same species. Bugs create more bugs, people birth more people, and every living creature strives to make life just like it is. We like combining spiritual energy with ourselves to form physical and fundamental spiritual energy. We like the combination of our spiritual power, our souls, energy fused with physical matter, and our bodies so much that we continue to make more of ourselves. You might ask what about mean and evil people? They want to make people just like themselves.

There is a spiritual theorem about attraction that states like attracts like. The forces of good and love are slowly building pressure on every inhabitant of the earth to radiate these same feelings. The world has a heartbeat. It's called the Schumann Resonance. All life on Earth supposedly vibrates at the same frequency. The Schumann Resonance historically beat steadily at 7.83 Hz until about four years ago. Then it began speeding up to speeds between 15 Hz to 25 Hz levels. It has even reached 36 Hz recently. Scientists tell us that this type of change is happening in our entire solar system.

This evolution of our world and solar system is a wakeup call to upgrade our ability to feel and express love. The vibration of the solar system is correlating closely to the higher energy frequencies of love and happiness. Now is an ideal time to choose love, joy, wisdom, and other positive feelings over anger, fear, and other negative emotions. We already have a great deal of information from the scientific community showing that the energy of love upgrades our biochemistry and well-being on all levels. As we allow ourselves to understand love more and feel it more consistently, we will enable our minds to use our brains to process information from our souls to improve our DNA. It will help us create more DNA strands and activate more brain cells. We will take a massive leap in our ability to accept and experience love. The times are changing. We will develop a new repertoire of advanced skills during the next few hundred years. We will create new ways to relax, heal, communicate with all of life, travel, and relate to other life forms. People have said we have entered the Age of Aquarius for the past 75 years. It appears as if they are right.

Confusion is spreading throughout the world at present. Wars are ongoing; governments are dictating the behavior of their people in many countries. New kinds of diseases are forming and scaring people, and governments are forcefully controlling their people. The people are resisting the pressures from their governments. It appears to be the rising of Aquarius. You can be the one who plants the seed for building a more loving, honest, and robust society for your friends and family. It will not be easy, but the saying goes, "Nothing worthwhile is ever easy." We are not in a time where change for the better will be easy because unhappy souls worldwide have a stranglehold on the behavior of other people. But the more people resist and stand up for their rights, the harder it gets for the unhappy and dishonest souls governing them to resist the pressure to give people their right to enjoy freedom and happiness. Many spiritual people are developing the wisdom that enables them to repel those that seem to want to control and oppress society.

As spiritual people, we can practice thankfulness, practice self-love, and express our appreciation for what we see as positive in our lives. This will not only help us, but will allow us to be an example for others. We can live a life full of joy or misery. It is our choice. When we take control of our emotions and practice mindfulness, gratitude, and spiritual love toward ourselves and others, we not only grow spiritually and improve our lives in this lifetime, but we also improve the lives of future generations.

THOUGHTS

- Empaths often become spiritual
- There are many definitions of love
- Love should never leave you exhausted
- Love should heal you
- To love others, you must love yourself
- Take responsibility for your feelings
- Love is a state of being
- Self-love is not selfish
- Our time on Earth prepares us for our future lives

CHAPTER 8
THE PATH TO WISDOM

IT IS GOOD TO BE INTELLIGENT. IF YOU ARE SMART, YOU likely know how to spell, read, and maybe even do mathematics. That is, if someone took the time to teach you about these things. There are a lot of supposedly intelligent people in the world. Look at all the politicians who are supposed to be smarter than their peers. They work in the government and, supposedly, make laws that help people. I've noticed few governments do anything which improves the life of the people they govern. They take care of the people in the government. They overtax their people, go to war with other countries, and make laws that help themselves rather than the citizens they are supposed to govern. They suppress their people and occasionally get caught in unlawful behavior. Many years ago, I joined a society that was only open to supposedly intelligent people. I'm not sure why they let me in. After a few months, I began noticing they were much like a cross-section of the public. Some of them could not get jobs, others were constant complainers about the current state of the world, and some enjoyed proving how smart they were by pointing out the mistakes everybody else made. I realized how easy it is to see other people's mistakes. Some people seem happy to point out how stupid other people are.

After that experience, I decided being intelligent was not as wonderful as you would believe. These people were just like everyone else. I decided it is better to be wise than bright. An intelligent person can still make stupid decisions, but a wise person usually makes excellent decisions. Every person on earth is a spiritual being. It behooves every living human who wants a future existence filled with love and joy to develop wisdom about accomplishing what they want in life. Possibly the best way is to make lots of mistakes when you are young. Other ways to build wisdom are thinking about the effects of people's actions, imitating wise people, and studying ways to succeed with your interests.

At this time in history, more and more people realize they are spiritual beings wrapped in human bodies. Being spiritual does not signal you are religious or even intelligent, although many religions claim they have the answers to get to heaven. Many spiritual people don't believe there is a place called heaven. They think we live eternally, going to different places and dimensions throughout eternity. Developing the ability to make wise choices is one of the main reasons for them spending time on Earth. You can enjoy your stay on Earth if you learn to make the right decisions. You can create the wisdom to make excellent decisions for yourself in several ways. As long as you keep your ability to make wise decisions, you are likely to lead a good life.

New experiences introduce new knowledge. Do you remember the first time you visited a zoo? Did you see an elephant for the first time and stand in wonder while watching the giant beast with the long nose? Seeing that elephant and all the other animals for the first time was probably a mind-expanding experience for you. It didn't make you any more intelligent, but it gave you a frame of reference for future dealings with animals. Knowing what they look and act like is your first step in acquiring wisdom about them. You developed a little understanding of animals. Always encourage yourself to be curious and keep an open mind about what you are experiencing.

Refuse to prejudge situations before they happen. Keep your mind open, and although you don't know what to expect, allow yourself to relive your childhood and look at every new situation as a learning experience in which you can learn something new. Dreading or worrying about an upcoming situation wastes time and can negatively affect you. Negative thoughts are stressful and not good for the soul. When you can look for pleasurable experiences or treat upcoming adventures with enthusiasm or an open mind, you grow in wisdom by soaking up the changes and possibly new ideas, while not setting others below or above yourself. Let new experiences become a regular part of living for you.

Many people don't ask questions when they have fresh adventures. There was a story about John Doe, born in 1920 and died in 1938. He got buried at age 65. The story's point was that John quit learning as soon as he graduated from high school. When he stopped learning, he was as good as dead. He was breathing for the rest of his life, but he might as well have been dead because he didn't bother to learn anything new. Learning should never stop during your time on earth. Many people over the ages of 75 or 90 continue to learn and credit their ability to learn as a significant thing that keeps them alive. You should never stop learning, even if you are a teacher or an expert. Wise people question everything. They question widely accepted knowledge, their own knowledge, and even the motivations of others that profess to be experts.

Earth life is a series of adventures that take us through many situations from which we can learn. The people who develop wisdom continue to learn. Most people reach a learning plateau at a young age and choose to remain in it. That is a lethal choice. Besides asking questions, when you share your knowledge, you also deepen your understanding because your mind can reconsider what you know and organize it better so you can explain it more clearly. Another thing about asking questions is that you control the conversation, because whoever you are conversing with needs to respond or communication stops. You will often improve friendships through questions because when they answer, you can see their point of view and understand them better. Enhancing your ability to understand people better helps you develop wisdom.

It is also good to slow down and relax or meditate at least once a day. Take a few minutes to relax and step aside from the rest of the world. Give yourself some time so you can just be yourself. When one is constantly busy and incessantly worrying about everything, it may make them appear devoted, conscious, and responsible, but it doesn't make them wise. Every day, spend a few minutes focusing on the practical and not-so-practical activities around you from an outsider's point of view. Digest what the unhurried perspective brings to you. Fill your free time with happy thoughts, learning something, or manifesting for your better future.

Wise people often know the answers better than anyone else, but they also know when to remain quiet. It is not always mandatory for them to voice their opinion just because they have one. When other people have suggestions on how to solve a problem, the wise person will often listen and even allow the ideas of others to be activated, even if they believe they have a better answer. They want everyone around them to be enlightened. They realize they do not have a monopoly on wisdom or knowledge. Spiritually, as for humans, one of our essential missions while on Earth is to develop personal insight and learn to exist in harmony with others. When people insist on being the one who always solves problems, they may very well interfere with the spiritual growth of others. If your opinions, thoughts, and ideas are necessary, give them. But it's also important to listen to people to understand what they say. The idea is to be receptive to the views of others and be a good listener. Wise people are good listeners.

Jeremy was in his late forties and the owner of a small gift shop when he hired David, a young man in his twenties. After David had worked for six months, Jeremy noticed his monthly sales had increased by about 50 percent. He also saw some new people turned into regular customers and often wanted David to help them. Jeremy did what any wise person would do and watched what David was doing to make so many sales and have such happy repeat customers. He noticed it always excited David to talk to his customers. He never pressured them, and always ensured they were happy with their purchases before they left. Jeremy did several things. He gave David a raise, complimented him about how he was so successful in dealing with people, and began emulating him in how he treated people. His sales also improved. David was new in sales, his employee, and 20 years younger than Jeremy. Jeremy didn't care about any of that. He found a winner he could learn something from and appreciated it. He was wise to do so. It helped him improve his business, and he also improved the way he handled his own customers. He was wise.

When you find people you respect and who do a better job than you do in any endeavor, you will be wise to emulate them. Look for people you can learn from who do the same things as you. Get to know them and question them about what they do and how they do it. Listen carefully to what they say so you can learn from their experience. These people do not have to be older, more intelligent than you, or even in your same field of work. Your mentors don't need to know they are mentoring you. They don't have to be close to you. You don't even need to like them. There might only be one or two things you want to learn from them. The wisest person you know might be a hairstylist, a bartender, or even your grandfather. Learn to recognize the wisdom coming from everyone.

Wisdom also comes from reading. Humankind has been inhabiting Earth as humanity for about 300,000 years. It took us many centuries to learn to read. The ability to read spread only after the invention of the printing press in the 15th century. Wise people very often are inveterate readers. They read everything they can get their hands on, from history and science books to comics. They dive into the writings of philosophers and the daily newspapers. If they have a library card, they will use it, their computers, and other online devices to find information. Wise people read about their particular field of work, hobbies, and anything that piques their interest. They are not above reading dictionaries and encyclopedias in their spare time. They will even read about other people's experiences to learn how to deal with situations they might face.

Health-wise, wise people are like spiritual people, and many intelligent people are spiritual. They don't just hunker down and hide from the world when they get sick or down in the dumps. They will talk to anyone who might know how to solve their problem. They are not fussy about with whom they share their concerns. They will go to a doctor, a lawyer, the little old lady who lives down the block known as a reiki practitioner, or anyone they feel knows how to help them. They surround themselves with willing and receptive people who can give them sound advice.

They are also down-to-earth, humble, and regular people. Often, famous people or influential people like politicians, doctors, and lawyers act like they are better than others. Wise people do not act like that. Generally, they are humble, relaxed, and always ready to help others in need of their services. They typically love what they get involved in and are happy to share with others. They are realistic and empathize with all that is good in themselves and you. When you are with another wise person, you will bring out the best in them, and they will bring out the best in you. I say another wise person because people who pursue this type of information are usually above average in wisdom. It takes a willingness to study and think to involve oneself in the study of spiritual energy or spirituality. Just reading this book is a sign that you either are wise right now or are on the road to becoming wise. Wise people accept their limitations and don't hesitate to learn from others or replicate the actions of others. They are natural, approachable, and decent people. They are reliable, respectable, genuine, and approachable because they consciously, or unconsciously, know these qualities work.

Wise people are like wizards, although they don't wear long robes with stars and planets on them, pointed hats, and hang out in caves, as you see in comic books. They are everyday people, and they love to share their wisdom. Many are spiritual people and models of what each of us should strive to become. They differ from many intelligent people in that they use their intelligence to make excellent, helpful decisions, while other supposedly smart people don't do anything to make their intelligence useful.

Wise people are models for each of us. The first thing we can learn from them is to look within to find our own faults. Many spiritual people do this when they go through the dark night or abyss, a time of terrific hurt and inner self-examination. They do lots of shadow work. That is self-examination to figure out what they are doing right and wrong and what is good in their life and what is not. Their aim is to find perfection while knowing they will never reach the ideal because perfection changes. They work on their beliefs to find out what views, biases, and opinions they have that are wise or not intelligent. Knowing yourself opens the door for you to grow and forgive yourself as you journey through life. Admitting that you are no better or worse than anyone else gives you the confidence and strength to treat others as equals and the power to stand above those who would treat you as beneath them. You will stand above them because they will still play games with you, and you will be above that type of nonsense.

Wise people accept the truth they cannot know everything. Look outward and see the many changes, improvements, and destructive happenings today. It is constant, and there are always new things to learn for those interested. You must never lose your curiosity and love for learning. The more you think about people, places, things, and events, the more you understand there is more to know. Wise people accept the idea that their knowledge is limited. Just because you know how to build a beautiful swimming pool does not mean you know how to fly an airplane. Wisdom comes with knowing much about a lot of things. Not just one thing. Wise people are responsible people. They know and accept they must be accountable for their thoughts, words, and actions. They develop their standards and live by them. They understand that living to satisfy the rules and standards of other people does not help them express their true selves because by following other people's rules, they allow others to determine their path through life. That is one powerful reason wise people often stray from religious life to follow their spiritual path. Wise people think for themselves and create their standards, which usually end up being higher than your everyday person's. They do their best to live where they are comfortable and do work that doesn't force them to compromise their compassion, interests, or ego.

Many people believe they are doing the right thing by keeping busy pursuing just about anything that will keep their minds off the world's troubles. They grow up believing adult work is essential and must be complex, laborious, and unsatisfying. The stress of their work life can make them feel important, but it can also be a distraction from knowing themselves and dealing with the essential issues in life. When they stay busy working, they don't do what the wise person does, like questioning their purpose in life, what life is all about, and why there is such a thing as life, anyway. Wise people do their best to keep their lives simple, harmonious, and flowing. Almost everyone has heard the slogan KISS, or "keep it simple, sweetheart." Wise people do their best to live by that slogan, although they are brilliant. As you become better at any endeavor, it should become easier for you to understand and accomplish it. If you work at it for months and months and it does not get easier or more enjoyable for you, you may be pursuing something wrong for you. Go within and focus on what you want out of life and what you want to do. Remember, you are a spiritual being spending time on Earth to learn new things and build up your ability to experience love and joy so you can carry them with you throughout eternity. You don't have to be the most intelligent person in the room to be wise. If you are willing to attempt it, you can tap into that special place within yourself. Being wise can save you a lot of pain, negativity, and heartache.

Be careful of any self-improvement advice that says it is easy. It isn't easy. Changing habits is never easy. Once you are on the road to self-improvement and have been doing it for a few months, it becomes habitual. Then it becomes easy because it has become your way of life. However, most people who seriously do shadow work say it is difficult, but also the most rewarding thing they ever do. As you understand any topic or activity better, you grow wiser in that area. Many people are intelligent in one area of their life, but not so smart in other areas. They are the first to speak up, usually pointing out mistakes others make. Mistakes are easy to see. Wise people know pointing out the mistakes of others does not make them look intelligent. They do it only when they feel it is necessary to help someone and not to criticize them. They think before they speak. Before they talk, they make sure it is not something they will regret saying later. They know once they say something, it is out, and they can't take it back. So, they always ensure that whatever they say is something they can be proud to admit they said if they are asked about it later.

They also know there is never a right time to accomplish something. They refuse to use excuses like, "When we get a new house," "When the kids are grown," or "When I get a new job" because they are wise. People use these common statements to rationalize the delay in doing things they think they want to do. The wise person's mantra is, "Let's do it now or as quickly as possible" if something delays the start of their efforts. Wise people know that putting off their dreams and goals only makes them older and not more intelligent.

Most people allow other people's behavior, emotions, and words to affect them. As a result, they allow other people's negativity to make them miserable. When you become upset, the other person wins, and you get stupid. However, when a wise person, or the people around them, get upset, they acknowledge that tension interferes with everyone's ability to receive intelligent thoughts from their soul. They do their best to relax themselves and everyone before they tackle the problem. They know the best decisions are made under harmonious circumstances. Wise people will do something like crack a joke or change the subject for a little while to help themselves and everyone else calm down. They are wise because they think for themselves. They have developed the ability to reason about everything in their life. As a spiritual person, you must become wise during your time on Earth to carry it with you as you transcend to the next dimension.

Keep your power by maintaining your calmness and joyful demeanor. You are needed to help build a better world filled with love, joy, trust, harmony, and advancement.

THOUGHTS

- So-called intelligent people are just like everyone else
- Think before you speak
- There is never a right time to start something
- Refuse to accept the status quo blindly
- Have a purpose or set a goal for yourself
- Accept other people for who they are
- Allow other people to speak their ideas
- Ask lots of questions
- Develop a do-it-now attitude

CHAPTER 9
THE SPIRITUAL WAR WITHIN

THROUGHOUT THE HISTORY OF THE UNIVERSE, THERE has been a war between positive and negative spiritual energies. When we look across the Universe, we can see discord, such as worlds colliding, comets disappearing, and even consistent weather changes here on Earth. When looking at the history of the world, we see that over the centuries, times have improved even though there has been a significant amount of unhappiness and conflict.

Many researchers claim humanity first appeared as tiny sponges and fishlike creatures that had to struggle to survive. There were rough seas that could easily wash us ashore, where we would expire from dehydration. Our souls were more extensive than us, and we had to learn to function within our physical bodies. From the very beginning, our souls suffered tremendous stress. We had to escape the attacks of our larger rivals to evolve into small land creatures. Slowly, over millions of years, we developed into mammals that looked somewhat like apes and monkeys. Finally, scientists believe the first mammals to take on human form evolved about 130,000 years ago. We began communicating with each other through the use of grunts and emotions around 32,000 years ago and have only had an alphabet to make words since about three or four thousand years ago. As our ability to communicate with words and writing eased our struggles, our negative behaviors have slowly declined, although there has always been a dichotomy of souls. Some want to exist in love, joy, and harmony, while others have a comfort zone of anger, disharmony, and distrust.

We have continually engaged in wars, personal vendettas, and other destructive behaviors ever since we first arrived on earth. But as time has passed, we live longer and have become healthier, more affluent, better educated, and safer from war. We see fewer murders, crimes, and accidents than in centuries past, and experience more love, harmony, and joy. We have experienced many victories in settling the differences between nations and the people in different countries. Our collective future appears to be bright despite the horrors of past centuries.

Because we are spirits, and because we have free will and make mistakes, this progress has not been even. Some nations have cruel dictatorships, and some governments are more moderate and allow more freedom. In every country, both evil people and caring, gentle people exist. The Universe, the total mass of spiritual energy in the Universe that many call God or Source, does not dither about our progress. This massive energy system is much like us; it will have places filled with love and joy and some filled with hate and anger. If you accidentally hit your left thumb with a hammer, it might hurt while your right thumb doesn't hurt. You are one person with many parts. And, just as in the spiritual universe, you don't have to hurt all over if one part of you hurts.

We've progressed because our emotions of love and joy are more potent than anger and hate. Spirits often develop what is called a comfort zone of negativity. They get used to expressing negative thoughts and feelings and they become part of their comfort zone. These feelings can be contagious, just like a cold or the flu. Other people pick them up, and the disharmony spreads. Also, a delightful and loving person can be contagious, and their vibrations will overcome those of negative people. Rational souls often make it a goal to improve the welfare of their fellow beings. They usually succeed when they apply their happy, loving thoughts and efforts to other sensible people. It often takes a great deal of time and effort.

Many people attempt to improve the tempers of others by criticizing their behavior. They end up spreading just the opposite of what they want to do. Their negative feelings, words, and thoughts spread out and contaminate the very people they want to improve. Their focus is so much on negative things they end up putting out negative energy. They often end up doing the very things about which they shout. Politicians are an example of a group who criticizes other people for the same things they are currently doing.

Progress has been slow over the years, but it continues to this day and will speed up in the future. We are going through a difficult period as the hostile forces work their hardest to pull everyone into harsh comfort zones. Fortunately, spiritual people are waking up and resisting them better than they ever have. While the loving souls used to give in to the cruel souls to keep the peace, they now realize it doesn't work, and are setting boundaries which will prohibit the hostile spirits from making the rules. It will not be easy, but loving souls will eventually win.

The future isn't as terrifying as some doomsayers might claim. We have good news to look forward to in the future. Beginning in the second half of the 19th century, life expectancy at birth rose from a historical average of around 30 years to the current average of 70 to over 80 years in the most fortunate countries. This gift of life is the hard-won dividend of advances in public health and education. We had advances such as the knowledge germs cause disease instead of other theories, such as foul smells, invisible spirits, conspiracies, and divine retribution. Things that helped us improve our health included ideas like safeguarding drinking water, inventions like the toilet and sewer systems, controlling diseases from insects such as mosquitoes and fleas, large-scale vaccination, and the promotion of handwashing. We have also developed many ways to improve primary prenatal and after-birth care, such as the encouragement of nursing.

When a virus or other disease causes a pandemic, advances in medicine keep them from killing as many people as they did in the era of folk healers and barber-surgeons. The advances in medicine during the past 50 years have been tremendous. Surgery has improved, transfusions are more common and safer, and we have more antibiotics and other chemicals to improve our health and delay death. The earth will become a place where spiritual entities can spend a few years practicing love, joy, and pleasure in innumerable ways. Some people would call it heaven or paradise. We will get there with the continual manifestation and effort of spiritual people.

Humanity has always needed food to survive. Initially, we struggled to grow and gather enough calories and proteins to feed ourselves. We started eating lots of wildflowers, fruits, weeds, and animals we could chase down. Today, the idea of the lack of nourishment is no longer valid in most parts of the world. It has been in decline in the last century. Starvation of the masses is only going on in the most remote areas and war-ravaged regions, of which there aren't many. The plentiful food supply comes from tremendous improvements in agronomy and the preservation of food.

For most of history, large parts of the world lived in poverty. In today's world, many people would classify medieval kings as living in poverty. Today, less than 10 percent of the population lives in extreme poverty. Even people in third-world countries have cell phones and other luxuries that no one even thought of as little as a hundred years ago. Our enrichment began during the Industrial Revolution, which started about 1760 and lasted until 1860. During that time, we learned to produce energy from coal, oil, wind, water, the sun, the earth, and even nuclear fission. Since then, our living conditions, ease of living, and ability to instigate positive change throughout our lives have improved steadily.

We used these fresh forms of energy to power machines we made, and we built huge factories to introduce mass production of goods to the world. We developed financial systems which helped us trade goods all over the world. Now we educate ourselves and our children to invent new ways to produce goods, enjoy ourselves, and learn to feel such qualities as love, gratitude, and joy. Yes, we still have wars, but they occur less often than in the Middle Ages. People are learning to get along, and the nations they live in are learning to live peaceably with each other.

One of the primary reasons nations get along better is because the people have better ways to communicate with each other and their governments. The people have asserted themselves to their leaders and told them they do not want to fight in wars. The populations in governments, either out of respect for the people they govern, or the desire to keep their jobs, are less interested in invading other countries. International trade also helped. It made it unwise to kill customers and debtors. People treat each other better, and unjust practices have declined in the past few years. Slavery is now verboten. They forbid it throughout the civilized world. We no longer tolerate human sacrifice and seldom apply corporal punishment. The world has banned the persecution of heretics and dissidents, and the oppression of women and religious, racial, and ethnic minorities. Of these negative injustices, not one has entirely become extirpated from the face of the earth, but each one has become more of a rarity than an everyday experience.

Moral progress in the past advanced through the struggle of spiritual people. A few well-known spiritual people had religions named after them, such as the Buddha and Jesus Christ. But the Buddha wasn't a Buddhist, and Jesus Christ wasn't a Christian. Now, people are breaking away from organized religion, and spiritual people are stepping up to instigate positive change. Our progress came about through the struggle of spiritual people. The powerful are never willing to hand over their privileges unless the strength of everyday people acting in solidarity takes it from them. Love, joy, and the power to make fair rules for everyone will continue to be effective and ultimately succeed. The abominable practices of today will become as outdated as the cruel tortures, slave auctions, and heretic burnings are to us today.

My friend Jerry Lee told me he never really appreciated anything until he was 40. He said he had to do without for several years before realizing many people helped make him the person he is now. He said he would always thank helpful people, but it was just a meaningless gesture to be polite. He wouldn't think about it any longer and didn't appreciate anything. He had some years where he had a tough time making a living for himself. The years when he did not prosper differed from the good years; it helped him realize how fortunate he was some people helped him. Jerry Lee said his whole life changed when he learned to appreciate people. He used to look for meanness and cruelty in the world, and he was the first to point out if someone made a mistake or did something wrong. Now Jerry Lee says that when someone makes a mistake, anyone can see it, and whoever made it usually knows it, so there is no need to point it out. It is much better to stand back and pitch in to help them fix it if they need help. Now he looks for good in everything and says he is much happier and more successful. Jerry is a spiritual person, and spiritual people like Jerry are bringing about positive changes in the moral fiber of the people on earth. We don't have to go out and work to convert everyone. Just being true to yourself will contaminate those around you. There can be positive contamination as well as negative contamination. That is how positive love, joy, and harmony spread. That is how it has been spreading for years. It has been slow because the necessity for survival brought more negative behavior about in past years.

Jerry Lee said it is easy to have gratitude. All you have to do is compare the good things that happen to you with the not-so-good stuff, and you can understand how they affect your life. When you can see and feel the difference, you will feel gratitude. Gratitude is one of the significant traits spiritual beings often develop during their stay on earth. You feel good when you are in tune with other spiritual beings. There is a lightness to it that feels warm and sensual. It makes you want to develop this warmth and harmony with other people, and you often will. When you build your unique charisma, you will draw people to you and create an elevated empathy for people. Because of your own experience with making mistakes and going through the turbulence of everyday life, you will develop an understanding of what other people go through. When people do things that would have hurt you or caused you anger at one time, it will no longer bother you as much. You will be calmer and manage them with more wisdom.

The time we spend as humans on earth is an opportunity to adjust our emotional behavior in ways that will help us during this lifespan and future lifespans. When we uniquely combine spiritual energy (our soul) and physical energy (our bodies), and learn to control them, we improve our ability to respond correctly to any situation.

Anger Is Contagious

The Universe's primary, original, fundamental, root, prime, vital, and necessary substance is spiritual energy. In the beginning, if there ever was a beginning, there was only energy. You may call this energy God energy, spiritual energy, or even subtle energy. Every cell of this primary energy carries knowledge and can change into other cell types. It also has eternal life. Since Plato's time, people debated the actuality of innate knowledge (knowledge brought with you from before you were born). However, it is becoming more and more accepted. Innate knowledge is like how a horse knows how to stand up and walk after it is born, with no one telling it how to walk. How does it know? It just knows, and we all have this type of knowledge. This energy with knowledge fills the Universe and combines with itself to form all other types of energy and matter.

Humankind is composed of God energy with soul energy and physical energy. Our physical energy is bones, blood, brains, and other parts of our bodies. God energy experiences everything we experience and accepts it. Soul energy also shares everything we experience. Soul energy instigates our thoughts, emotions, and our reactions. One significant unique feature of living on Earth as human beings is our ability to work with our physical and spiritual bodies to improve how we react to events. They multiply the strength and feeling of everything we meet exponentially more than when we are purely spiritual beings.

Typically, we respond to specific actions in the same way. Someone gives us a present, and we say thank you. Someone smiles at us, and we usually smile back. We believe someone is yelling at us, and we get mad and scream back at them. We think they're directing their scream at us when sometimes it is their way of expressing frustration. Our defensive and aggressive response triggers an argument when it isn't necessary. But because our souls control our thoughts, feelings, and activities, we can change and improve how we react to anything.

As spiritual people, we must remain calm in any situation, no matter how tense. We want to avoid being frustrated, which causes anger. We strive to win or feel content with the result of an argument. And if another person is involved, we want to keep their friendship or respect. Anger cuts off the blood flow to our brains and causes our souls' peaceful, loving thoughts to be misdirected and confused. It is unhealthy, as habitual anger can cause cancer and premature death. It will also hurt your friendships, work life, and other relationships.

Many people feel they have no control over their emotions. They get mad quickly and then feel stupid for getting angry when the situation is over. They got mad because they felt frustrated with the situation or felt trapped with limited options. Anger can be aggressive and defensive; anything can set some people off. It is also a way for people to avoid responsibility for their actions and feelings. Many of us have said something like, "He made me mad because of whatever." No. It was perhaps not even his intention to make you mad. He was concerned with his thoughts and feelings. Whoever he may be, he is frustrated. It does not mean you need to get angry with him, although anger can be contagious, just like a disease.

Understanding our anger, our trigger points, and how to overcome our anger gives us more understanding of other people's anger. We can have more empathy for those who get angry easily. Our anger tells us we are suffering from some distress. It can be a motivator or a deactivator. It can make us want to fight, or it can make us want to hide. It is very hard on us mentally, physically, and emotionally. It comes from frustration about not getting our way, rejection, or perceiving some threat. Unless you deal with it, it can lead to problems with relatives, depression, shame, drug addiction, and jail time if you get too far off the track.

Some people get aggressive when they are angry. Others deny their anger, and some turn it inward and hold it in. They refuse to admit their anger. Refusing to accept your anger can make you both mentally and physically sick. We can be born with a propensity to be angry. Sometimes we have anger carried over from our past lives and experiences. It can come from how our family members and other people treated us. If mistreated, there is a good chance of developing a default feeling of underlying anger. We could even pick it up from listening to the media, preachers, or politicians screaming and ranting about the bad guys. We sometimes manage our anger by burying it or taking it out on someone we associate with, which is unhealthy.

Anger usually flares up with a triggering event. Normally, it is something another person says or does. It may be a political decision that complicates your life or something another person does that frustrates you. It could be an event as simple as flies swarming around your face and bothering you, or a sudden illness. Any event you take as an adverse experience can trigger your anger, even if it is imaginary. You can get upset by upcoming events when you feel they won't go well. When things you expect to go wrong go wrong, it can infuriate you.

Learning to manage your anger is vital to free your soul so you can adjust to a life of peace and harmony instead of shame, hurt, and fear, which can bring wrath from other people. Meditation is potent in helping one become relaxed, calm, and focused. During meditation, you can separate yourself from the feeling of anger as you view your lapse into anger from afar. Sit outside yourself and calmly see your pain and suffering with relaxed calmness. View yourself with compassion, be sensitive to your feelings, have no self-pity emotions, and stabilize them. When you can look at yourself with compassion and understanding, it helps you smooth out your emotions and gives you more control. You can accept your feelings and change them to help you and not hinder you. Acceptance of self will heighten one's self-esteem and improve one's ability to avoid anger.

As spiritual creatures, we all have the ability to control our own emotional behavior. When we realize that emotions are contagious, we can do our part of raising the spiritual consciousness of the world simply by maintaining feelings of happiness, love, and harmony in all of our activities. Our first step is to discard every bit of anger we cling to.

THOUGHTS

- Our future is bright
- Love and joy are more potent than anger and hate
- We are better off than ever before
- Progress is uneven
- Negative words and thoughts are contagious
- The earth will become a place of love and joy
- We all have innate knowledge
- Learn to manage your anger

CHAPTER 10
DUMP THE ANGER

SINCE WE HAVE TO SPEND TIME ON EARTH ANYWAY, IT IS a good idea to keep our bodies healthy to accomplish what we want. When our bodies become damaged or sick, it makes it difficult to understand the desires and thoughts of our souls. Our soul is the animating force that keeps our body alive and well. It not only brings thought to us but also animates every organ of our body so they can adequately communicate with each other. When our organs get messed up, we get sick, and our ability to act as our souls tell us to work decreases. We get ill and lose some of our ability to understand what is happening around us. We may also lose our ability to communicate with other people.

You develop your soul as you learn the reasons for your hurts and fits of anger. Make a list of things and the behaviors that make you mad. When you recognize them, you can step back and change your behavior. You can change it so you will act to make you happy or even proud of yourself. Change your behavior, so you behave in ways that will help you lead a more comfortable, fulfilling, and productive life. As spiritual people, we already know we live in different states of being throughout eternity. We know we don't take our biological material with us through our many periods of existence. We are reasonably sure we eventually lose parts of our memories during our many periods of physical life. We also know our memories fade and often change during each lifetime. But our ability to think and experience emotion stays with us forever. Just as in our present life, our feelings and thoughts continually change as the spiritual energy surrounding us affects them. Our stay on Earth is a fantastic time to learn to overcome emotions like anger, hate, shame, frustration, and depression.

When people get angry, they pump blood at a rate not conducive to rational thought. It clogs the thought process and forces out confusing thoughts that increase the underlying anger and blocks an increased amount of intelligent thought. You are likely to do something stupid when you act under the pressure of anger. You often say things you regret only 20 or 30 minutes later. Screaming and venting your anger makes the situation worse. You might say you are at least getting it off your chest. But, in reality, you are only reinforcing your anger habit. When you focus on a negative emotion, you usually intensify the experience, making it more challenging to relax and get over it. Research on anger has shown that chronic irritation can cause problems in one's relationships and cause cardiovascular and heart problems. It is not scientifically proven yet, but many people believe chronic anger is a contributing factor to the development of cancer. People with bad tempers often have difficulty keeping their friends because most people don't enjoy being around people who might complain or argue.

Meditation will help you reduce your times of anger and will enable you to learn to relax and respond to your triggers the way you want to. Meditation is to engage in contemplation or reflection. It is the easiest way to teach yourself to focus your thoughts peacefully. When you want to change a habit, your soul, which is you as a spiritual being, decides what you want to change. You then transfer the idea to your mind, which carries it to your physical body. Then, hopefully, your body reacts to help you change the habit. It often takes coaching and nudging from you as your soul. You may need to relax and look at the situation objectively without evaluating it as good or bad or right or wrong. Initially, it may not be easy to contemplate a thought without feeling turbulent emotions. Still, by relaxing long enough over time, you will do it. The more you ponder about anything negative, the easier it will come and the less bite it will have on you. Be open to the experience, whether you like or dislike it. Directing our spiritual reality isn't always the easiest thing to do.

While you relax, analyze the reasons for your anger. Ask yourself what types of situations usually make you angry. Who, what, why, where, and when do you tend to become angry? Journal it. Relax and write it down whenever you lose your temper. Write about whatever made you mad. Write about whatever was the trigger that set you off. If it is one person, what is it about them that irritates you? You are going through a learning experience. It would be best if you learned something from your anger that will help you remain calm and relaxed in future times of stress. One solution is to avoid people or situations that trigger your anger. That is almost impossible because there is no way to know what you will experience in the future, especially if you get angry often.

When relaxed, you can study your feelings and actions as your anger develops. Once you see and understand them, you can recognize them in the future as warning signs you are on the road to being angry. Focus on things such as how you physically change as you get mad. Do you breathe faster, deeper, or harder, or do your muscles tighten up? How about your voice? Do you stutter, or do you quickly start raising your voice? Get a clear picture of yourself as you become triggered. See how you first react to the trigger and the expected results of the situation. When you meditate on what things set you off, you can learn what they are to recognize the signs when they show up in future cases. Say you catch yourself beginning to raise your voice, or your muscles tighten. Visualize yourself relaxing and feeling waves of happiness or calmness flowing through you.

Learning to calm yourself is a spiritual exercise. You are cooperating with yourself through your soul. Your spiritual self is helping you change your mental, physical, and emotional responses to unpleasant situations. While meditating, visualize a situation where you got angry. Picture it as clearly as possible. You can become mad while doing this; it will be even better if you get angry. Instead of focusing on your anger, focus on the sensations in your body. Focus on the flushing of your face, your heavy breathing, and your possible tight muscles. You might even feel a tightness in your stomach or chest area. Treat this situation much like you change old, unhappy memories. Think about it the same way you think about getting rid of some dirty old clothes. Visualize the problem as you would like to treat any similar condition. See yourself relaxing and being able to think with wisdom. See yourself the moment you feel anger coming on, relaxing and calmly deciding about what to do or say.

The anger you experience causes pain to your physical self and is a spiritual expression. It is just as painful to your spiritual self as your physical self. Suppose you continue to react with anger to stuff that doesn't please you during this life. In that case, you will most assuredly have the same propensity to respond in the same manner during your next incarnation, no matter your dimension or location. During this life on Earth, your existence is an excellent time to develop yourself the way you want to exist for the rest of eternity. We all have free will. The choice is ours. We can learn to live successfully and happily and filled with love. We can live with anger, regret, envy, distrust, hate, and any other destructive emotion we wish to keep.

When you review your moments of anger, view your feelings and thoughts like they are coming from someone else. Stop and listen to your words. Notice how inappropriate they are. Relax and calmly observe them as if watching a bonfire or an action movie. Your anger will probably pull you away from your thoughts, which is okay. Just pause, relax again, and return to the scene of your anger. Focus on the sensation you feel and change the setting in your mind to one where you think you learned a wonderful lesson. Picture the love and happiness you can generate and feel it. Do this for 15 to 20 minutes a day until your feelings of anger subside. As you do this activity over and over, it will be easier and easier to do. You can do this with any emotional behavior you want to change about yourself.

When you are angry, you experience changes in your thoughts, emotions, and physical body. When you first feel any of these signs you want to change, consciously take a few deep breaths until you feel normal again. Focus on your breath and feel the air slowly going down to your diaphragm and out again. Remember to step back from your role as a participant into your role as an observer. Remember, you do not need to be upset. Refrain from judging or blaming anybody for anything. Just label what happens as a scene in a play or movie. There is no reason you have to get upset. It is your job to observe and make excellent decisions about what is happening.

Another seldom-mentioned method of combating your anger is to hum as soon as you feel irritation. Humming produces vibration throughout your lungs, nose, and throat. The beat is much like meditation, as it helps you relax. When you begin to feel anger during a confrontation, your humming will very likely cause a distraction. The sound has a spiritual effect on you and everyone else who hears it. The vibration of the hum sends a spiritual message to everyone who hears it, but almost no one will understand it. Human beings have largely lost the power to communicate with each other spiritually. As human beings, we have only been able to form words for about 50,000 years. Before that, we spoke with grunts, made guttural sounds, and displayed emotions. We communicated in our ancient history much like our pet animals, such as cats and dogs, communicate with each other today. Many people speak of animals as not knowing how to think like humans, but it is pretty easy to see they know when you are happy, mad, sick, or healthy. It may be questionable if our speaking ability has improved our communication ability over the years.

When you hum, it distracts you from your anger because you will concentrate on the humming rather than on what you are mad about. If you are in a confrontation, it will distract whoever you are confronting or whoever is confronting you. Your humming may further anger your antagonists, or they may stop everything and ask you what or why you are doing the humming. Whatever they do, you have changed the situation's dynamics, allowing you to settle down and keep your wits about yourself. If they ask you what or why you are humming, you can be honest with them and tell them you were getting angry and didn't want to be angry. Be honest and tell them you want to think calmly. This might actually throw them completely off their anger and create a state of puzzlement for them. There is an excellent chance they will become amicable and discuss the situation rather than argue with you.

You can always control the conversation by asking questions. When you ask another person a question, it pressures them to respond. Some people will ignore you, but you can keep asking them questions, and they will eventually have to react. You can ask questions like, "Why do you feel that way? Are you upset? Do you know this conversation is making me upset? Are you upset about something?" Or you can go way off base and bring up a completely different subject. Ask a question like, "Do you have a dog?" Or maybe something silly such as, "Do you think the stars that shine at night turn off in the daytime?"

Another example might be, "Do you know who your father is? Or do you know what the capital city of Utah is?" These questions break up the flow of an accelerating situation. Changing the subject with a question so far from the subject matter will throw the anger-causing situation into a new frame of reference. They give you time to settle down and usually throw your antagonist off their thought pattern.

Anger is simply an uncomfortable and often harmful state of mind. It is a warning, and over time, it causes unnecessary stress to your body and leads to nothing good. There is always something that triggers anger. It can be something that upsets you, something like embarrassment, shame, provocation, and especially frustration. You might get angry at a family member, a friend, or an event, such as getting stuck in traffic. Memories of past traumatic events can also cause present anger. You may harm yourself, your family, or anybody when you get out of control because of anger. It is difficult to guess the outcome of uncontrolled anger. Painful emotions close off the pathways of rational thought; almost anything can happen, and all results are alarming.

Over the years, there have been millions and millions of beatings and deaths resulting from uncontrolled anger. It can be terrifying to be around someone who loses control of themselves. Some people get so angry that everyone around them will want to leave the scene. Uncontrolled anger can be so unhealthy that the stress caused by the rage will drain the angry person and everyone in the area. It leaves no room for harmony or satisfaction. It causes fear and loathing. On the other hand, showing anger in a controlled manner during a negotiation may increase one's ability to succeed. Show that you are unhappy, but do so calmly. A person's natural response when frustrated and angry is to get angrier. Then they get aggressive, develop horrible feelings, shout, curse, or maybe even turn inward and pout. As said earlier, a violent reaction may negatively impact your health, or you might harm others or yourself. Once you learn what causes your anger and recognize it, you can express it healthily. You can calm yourself, analyze the situation, and speak your piece pleasantly. It always benefits you to keep any confrontation on a level of comfortably understandable messages.

Almost everyone has heard that when you feel angry, take a deep breath and settle down. Taking deep breaths might work, but you may need to take 20 or 30 or maybe 200 deep breaths. Some people will probably need to take a thousand breaths. Refuse to react to the situation until you relax and get your wits about you. Remember that the moment you show your anger is when everything goes downhill. Deep breathing and settling down will often give you time to think straight. Doing something physical to help you calm down, like going for a walk or chopping wood, is also helpful. Do anything that makes you use your body and muscles.

Physical Activity Helps You Cool Down

Physical activity stimulates your mind and various hormones, making you feel happier and relaxed. When you succeed at calming yourself, you can respond in a kind but assertive and noncontroversial manner. At this time, make your concerns and needs known clearly and directly without trying to hurt anyone. Find and explain what upsets you. Looking for the cause of your displeasure and asking your antagonist to help you resolve it is a wise and spiritual way of fixing it. You are asking for and will probably receive understanding and cooperation. Most people continue the argument until everyone tires of yelling at each other, and nothing gets resolved the way it should. When you settle down and approach the situation in a relaxed, friendly manner, you set the tone for a cooperative conversation. Often, the matter can get settled amicably.

When you follow this step, the outcome is usually a pleasant one. Never blame another person for your anger. When you get mad, it is on you and no one else. Blaming other people for your anger is a cop-out. You oversee your emotional behavior. When we criticize and complain about other people causing our rage, it doesn't help anyone. It makes us look like whiners and usually only aggravates the situation. When you hold on to your anger, it is as if you drink poison to punish the other person for irritating you. There is no reasonable excuse to harm oneself for the crimes of someone else. Treat the person you are angry with as respectfully as you expect them to treat you. You likely will get respect and appreciation back. Very few people like to be in confrontational situations. When we return to our spiritual reality, most want to experience love, joy, and creativity. Getting rid of any inclination to engage in anger is essential for supporting happiness.

Be honest and acknowledge you are the only person who can control your temper. Everyone has different beliefs and experiences which form their beliefs. We all have mental and emotional quirks, thoughts, and needs. Each of us has different feelings and coping abilities. It is often a shock when someone learns that not everyone has the same ability to understand information as they do. This lack of comprehension often causes anger. Lack of understanding is why it isn't fair and justifiable to expect agreement from others and that their behavior should be precisely like yours. In most tense situations, you will be the one to start the steps to tone down the tension. And once you develop this ability, your self-esteem will grow.

Most people won't think about doing it or even know it's possible. Sometimes someone will do something or say something that hurts you terribly. When people say hurtful things, they often do it unintentionally and without forethought. Often, they don't mean to do it. Being hurt or unintentionally insulted has happened to most people at least once or twice in their lifetime.

Some people seem to make it a hobby by going from relationship to relationship and getting hurt in every one of them. They will befriend someone and become very close to them in weeks. Then the other party accidentally or unintentionally dumps all over them and refuses to see them anymore. Then they hurt and develop a grudge against the person who left. When someone you have been very close to suddenly dumps you, it can be a heartbreaker and hard to overcome. When this happens, it is good to relax as best you can and accept that the relationship is not there anymore. Then it is a good idea to start brainstorming to figure out what new doors can open for you. What did you do in the past when you were in a situation where things didn't work out? If you have never been in a similar position before, focus on how to replace the relationship. What can you do to enjoy something that you have never done before?

Anger, resentment, and anxious thoughts can overwhelm you. Your physical body can't run away and protect itself from your thinking. Your body becomes victimized by your thoughts, which project inward. This anger becomes poison you put into your physical form through your soul. Now the person or situation you think you direct these thoughts towards will survive to enjoy another day while you take the poison. Think of each negative thought as a glass of poison. It brings a state of disease. A state of disease then gets transferred into your physical body. You can think your way into a state of discomfort and illness. It is not so easy to think your way out of it.

Thoughts are real. Thoughts are as honest as anything you will ever know. Stop poisoning yourself. Think about simply allowing yourself to feel love and becoming a spiritual expression of love. People spend little time developing their knowledge about love. They hook up with someone, and whatever their relationship is, they call it a loving relationship, even if one constantly abuses the other. It usually takes some wisdom to understand and appreciate love. Governments and religions have made different rules to define love. In many places, a person can only love one other person. Also, people are supposed only to love their children or parents. At one time, the parents chose the marriage partner. In the early days of humanity, they didn't worry about love. When people reached the age where they could reproduce, they just had sex and didn't worry about anything so mundane as love. They lived in small groups and cooperated in ways that would help them survive. Enough survived that we became civilized and built cities, states, and governments. Now we are at the stage where we can learn about love, happiness, harmony, and how we relate to our souls. Spiritually, love is a feeling. When you love someone, you want what is best for them, and you want to act in harmony with them. And as spiritual beings, you can love whoever and whenever you want. You will love no one more than you love yourself. Love is the ultimate expression of your soul.

THOUGHTS

- Keep your body healthy
- Anger interferes with rational thought
- Emotions are a form of communication
- Anger can make you sick
- Physical activity can help you relax
- Recognize anger when you first feel it
- You can control a conversation with the use of questions
- Learn to live with the feeling of joyful love

CHAPTER 11
FIND YOUR MAGIC

PEOPLE ACCEPT THE IDEA THAT WE LIVE IN THE UNIVERSE. People also believe the Universe has other worlds, comets, planets, and many diverse objects scattered within its borders. Not universally accepted is the idea that everything in the Universe is energy that constantly vibrates, flows, has knowledge, and changes form. Nobel Prize-winning scientists such as Einstein, Bohr, and others have proven the idea that energy is everything many times. We are used to thinking about everything in the Universe as tangible, liquid, solid, or gas. Accepting the idea that everything is just energy can be challenging.

During the last 100 years, quantum physicists discovered our physical "reality" consists of atoms. The atoms in our bodies are numerous vortexes of spinning and vibrating energy similar to a tornado; how we perceive this energy as a solid, liquid, or gas depends on the atom's speed. Looking at an atom under a microscope, we will see an invisible tornado of vibrating energy. When we focus on the structure of the atom, it becomes clear all that exists is a void. As atoms don't have form, everything that is physical isn't solid. That means we, as humans, are made from something that isn't solid. We can touch and feel ourselves, but they tell us we aren't solid. That is a wild idea. The idea that humans are made from atoms, and are not invisible, can get very technical. The neutrons in each atom dance. They dance so fast they appear solid, and we have so many of them, they feel solid. Teeming particles are a simplified version of why everything tangible appears solid. This is not only difficult to understand but also difficult to explain.

Even though everything in the Universe looks different, it all comes from the same energy. It just vibrates at different speeds that give it the appearance of being solid. Then why does it hurt when you cut through your skin, like with a paper cut? Scientists say the paper separates the energy of the skin and reveals nerves that are exposed to the outside world and get angry. Everything exists at different frequencies, making it tangible or intangible, solid, or not. Our existence as a human is a heavy topic. The energy that vibrates slowly is on the lower end of the spectrum and is dense and tangible; energy that vibrates quickly is light and intangible and vibrates on the higher end. Our human form vibrates at slower wavelengths in the entire scheme of the Universe. We exist at a slower frequency, which is why we perceive ourselves as physical, tangible beings. We are still a mass of energy. According to quantum physics, humans have no actual physical structure. We are vibrational patterns of spinning vortices of interactive energy, each with a unique signature. This signature makes us all different from one another.

We feel separated from everyone and everything because our energy vibrates differently than everything else. Everything connects and communicates with the divergent energies here on earth and the incoming energies from different parts of the Universe. This information is deep but will help us relate to our place in the Universe. The Law Of Movement and Vibration states that everything in the Universe consists of energy that vibrates at different speeds. Although many people are naturally sensitive to spiritual energy, others become attuned to it the more they become open to the messages from their higher consciousness. When conscious awareness is strong, we can tap into incoming energy wavelengths and read the information stored within them. This energy can guide us and ultimately lead us to reach our full potential and higher purpose.

We can tell if we are sensitive to spiritual energy when we recognize how we feel around other people. When you are around people who help you feel relaxed, comfortable, and good about yourself, you pick up good energy from them. Conversely, you may feel uncomfortable or nervous when you pick up a negative vibe from others. However, anyone going through a period of depression or a dark night might feel uncomfortable around people who want to help them. While spiritually hurting, our thoughts often become muddled. Empathetic people or empaths may notice they regularly feel susceptible to spiritual energy or believe they feel "too much." This sensitivity can cause them to withdraw or lock down their emotions because they don't want people to accuse them of being overly emotional. All that is happening is they are aware of everything taking place in their immediate—or distant—environment and are soaking it all up. When we can sense and read the energy that radiates from others, we can also sense energy from the Universe. We might often feel telepathic or "know" things with no logical explanation and then find it difficult to explain the source of our information to others.

We might also notice we often feel as if we're on an emotional rollercoaster when we take on everyone else's emotions. Taking on other people's emotions may cause us to become moody and irritable, experience headaches, avoid going to specific places, or refuse to spend time with certain people. It is essential to remain alert when we feel any sudden changes to our emotional or mental state so we can quickly separate and identify which emotions belong to us and which are coming from others. This is easy to do. Say you have an acquaintance who you are not friendly with. In fact, you don't like them, and you get upset when you think about them. The emotions you feel then are coming from you. When you get around them, although you aren't happy there, your emotions change for the worse. The emotions will appear to come from them. When you enter a room with a few people in it and you become emotionally elated or tense, you are probably picking up the emotional flavor of the people in the room. But you could also suddenly become elated or dejected because of someone you see. The more attention you pay to your own emotions, the easier it is to do.

We should conduct a similar process when receiving incoming energies from the outer realms so we do not absorb feelings that may lower our vibration and cause us harm. We can vividly sense other people's energy because thoughts, feelings, emotions, and motivations emit electromagnetic waves, which we can feel in our electromagnetic field, soul, and aura. Our sensitivity is part of why we can be empathetic towards other people, as when we attune to the frequency of these waves, we can clearly understand and quickly feel how other people are feeling.

Our sensitivities can cause us difficulties, which is why we must understand them. Difficulties may tempt us to close off our senses, but it is not the best solution. We will suffer from anguish and anxiety until we understand what is arousing the uncomfortable feelings. It is difficult to ignore energy because it will not disappear until you acknowledge it, understand it, and redirect it. Absorbing too much energy can overstimulate spiritual people and become emotionally draining and debilitating quickly, especially if we passively take it in without first protecting our energy field. The practices of meditation and mindfulness, spending time with nature, and keeping our minds positive can all help combat negative emotions.

Human beings have limitless potential and are capable of far more than people teach us to believe. The Universe constantly communicates with us by showing us synchronicities, signs, and symbols, and offering us a myriad of subliminal messages which can enhance our earthly experience. They appear as goosebumps, chills, shivers, visions, angel numbers, and dreams. Supposedly, it is impossible to receive communication through the mind from unknown sources, but we all have a certain amount of innate knowledge with which we were born. For example, babies automatically know to suckle their mother's breast and crawl. Many small children have memories of their past lives. We often get questioned about where we get our information, or we get criticized, or even told our data is incorrect. This abuse can cause us to lose faith in our intuition and psychic ability.

Many people are afraid of being psychic or perceived as psychic because of some ancient myths and tales of witchcraft or devils surrounding this ability. Fear will profoundly affect our ability to receive information. Fear will often block the flow and reduce the messages and sensations when our mind wants to be open and trusting. Whether we accept the incoming energy, flow with it, and unravel our destiny or reject it, the opportunity to access the infinite amount of data that universal energy carries is our choice to take or reject. We know this data as the global or collective consciousness. It explains how people simultaneously feel specific joy, depression, or a heavy sensation in the air when trauma, good things, or conflict occur.

Energy is universal and connects all matter and spirit. We have access to everything in the Universe. All we have to do is keep our vibration and awareness high and allow our intuition to make sense of all existing energy to which we have immediate access. We can do this simply by opening our minds, believing, welcoming, and feeling what the Universe tells us. The Universe is energy. The first law of thermodynamics states that energy cannot be created or destroyed, but it can be transformed from one form to another. The amount of energy and matter in the Universe stays constant, merely changing from one state to another. Energy is any source of usable power, such as fossil fuels, electricity, spiritual, subtle, Qui, or solar radiation. It is an interpersonal, physical, or non-physical force or essence. You are spiritual energy and will go through myriads of physical forms during your journey through eternity.

There Is no Separation Between Man and God

Scientists believe the Universe to be at least 10 billion light years in diameter and contain many galaxies; it has expanded since the Big Bang about 13 billion years ago. They considered the earth the center of the Universe for most of recorded history. But for most of history, people believed the Universe consisted only of those planets visible to the naked eye and an outlying sphere of fixed stars. No one ever positively knew where heaven and hell were. Heaven is supposedly located somewhere in the sky, but no one has pinpointed it yet. Hell is often said to be in the middle of the earth.

By the 20th century, observations revealed that the Milky Way galaxy was one of many billions in an expanding universe, grouped into clusters and superclusters. The earth is in the Milky Way galaxy. At the end of the 20th century, the visible Universe became more visible, with superclusters forming into a vast web of galaxies, voids, and planets. Superclusters, filaments, and voids are the most significant coherent structures in the Universe that we can see. At still more considerable distances, the Universe becomes homogeneous, meaning that all its parts have, on average, the same density, composition, and structure. It is still undetermined whether the Universe is finite or infinite. Scientists now speculate that a multiverse may exist, of which the known universe is only one example. However, there is no direct evidence of a multiverse.

We know the Universe has knowledge. Our ability to think proves there is at least some knowledge in the Universe. Look at it this way. The Judeo-Christian Bible says in the beginning was the Word, and the Word was with God, and the Word was God. So, many people say, in the beginning, there was God. Others say there was nothing or a mass of energy at the beginning. The energy is still around, so until proven wrong, it makes sense to say there was energy at its start. That energy can be called anything you want, whether it be God, the Word, or the Source. But whatever you choose to call this energy, it is filled with knowledge which is available to each of us.

The Universe appears like a colossal brain. At first glance, the human brain's neural network looks similar to the network of the physical universe, stretching throughout the vastness of space. Physicists Chen Ning Yang and Tsung-Dao Lee won the Nobel Prize for proving that subatomic particles have intelligence. Physicists have suggested for years the Universe may be a giant brain because it looks and behaves like one.

According to a study in *Nature's* Scientific Reports, "The universe may be growing in the same way as a giant brain, with the electrical firing between brain cells 'mirrored' by the shape of expanding galaxies." The way the Universe develops and runs appears much like a massive brain. Our minds are a microcosmic mind of the macrocosmic mind. Ancient esoteric teachings of Hermeticism state that All is Mind, and the Universe is Mental. In other words, God is the mind, and everything in it is connected. We are all part of this living mind and consciousness, which is the fabric of the Universe. There is no separation between humanity, the Universe, and what most people call God. Science is slowly finding truth in these ideas that have been with spiritual people for thousands of years.

Basic spiritual energy is like what is now called stem cells. It is like one humongous, invisible stem cell that can loosen its separate parts from itself while still keeping itself attached to everything with an ultra-thin, invisible membrane. It can turn portions of itself into anything and everything. The total energy of the Universe flows through all matter and forms every type of thought, emotion, matter, and structure. It generates everything in existence and connects its different parts through having different velocities, vibrations, thicknesses, flavors, and states of being. It is like a large room filled with steam. The steam in the room has the power to clump up into every imaginable thing in existence while still staying attached to every other drop of moisture. As one tiny drop of condensation would be a tiny part of the mass of steam, the total amount of steam would be incomplete without it. The Universe would be unfinished without you. You would be equal to every other drop of vapor in every way.

The earliest time pure spiritual energy formed new life forms on earth was over 4.5 billion years ago. There wasn't even an animal that looked like a precursor to humanity at that time, and there was very little oxygen to help animals maintain life. Besides the land, the earliest evidence of life on earth is microfossils about 3.5 billion years old. Over the past 5 billion years, over 99 percent of all life forms living on earth have become extinct. Science tells us there are currently 10 to 15 million different species now living on earth. They have documented over a million, and over 86 percent are still unknown. However, scientists estimated in a May 2016 report that there are over 1 trillion species living on earth, and only one-thousandth of 1 percent of them have been identified. Sponges are supposedly among the earliest animals. While compounds from sponges show up in rocks as old as 700 million years, molecular evidence points to them having developed even earlier. No one knows for sure exactly how old they are.

Oxygen levels in those early days were still low compared to today, but sponges can tolerate low-oxygen conditions. Although, like other animals, they require oxygen to metabolize. They don't need much because they are not very active. They feed while sitting still by extracting food particles from water pumped through their bodies by specialized cells. The simple body plan of a sponge consists of layers of cells around water-filled cavities supported by hard skeletal parts. The evolution of ever more complex and diverse body plans would eventually lead to distinct groups of animals. While not shown initially, there is evidence that instructions for complex bodies were present even in the earliest animals. Progress toward developing human bodies had already begun. The Universe, or God, continually creates fresh forms of life to experience.

By the end of the Ediacaran Period, which spanned from 635 million years ago to 538 million years, oxygen levels rose, approaching levels sufficient to sustain oxygen-based life. The early sponges may have helped boost oxygen by eating bacteria, which saved them from decomposing. Tracks of an organism named Dickinsonia (very early frogs and toads) suggest that the organism may have moved along the sea bottom, feasting on carpets of tiny microbes. However, about 541 million years ago, most Ediacaran creatures disappeared, signaling significant environmental change scientists are still working to understand. Evolving animal body plans, feeding relationships, and ecological engineering may have played a role in our early development. Burrows found in the fossil record, dating to the end of the Ediacaran Period, reveal that worm-like animals had excavated the ocean bottom. These early environmental engineers disturbed and maybe aerated the sediment, disrupting conditions for other Ediacaran animals. As ecological conditions deteriorated for some animals, they improved for others, potentially catalyzing a change-over in species.

The Cambrian Period, dating from about 485 to 541 million years ago, saw a wild explosion of new life forms. Along with unique burrowing lifestyles came complex body parts, like shells and spines. By using these body parts, animals could engineer their environments dramatically through hole digging instead of burrow scraping. The animals that formed became more active and started growing heads, arms, tails, and legs for directional movement to help them chase prey. Active feeding by well-armored animals like trilobites may have further disrupted the sea floor on which the gentle Ediacaran creatures had lived. By the end of the Cambrian Period, nearly all existing animal types or species (mollusks, arthropods, annelids, etc.) existed, and food webs were emerging, forming the foundation for the ecosystems on Earth today. Geologists say we are now in the Quaternary Period, which immediately followed the Cambrian Period.

In this period, people believe we differ from the energy of God or the Universe. We started as tiny creatures living in a liquid setting with only ozone to breathe. As time went on, we kept evolving to become animals that could survive breathing air. We learned to walk and talk and developed into the state we are in today. We started as spiritual entities and remain as spiritual entities today. It has taken us millions of years to build to our present stage, where we have cars, skyscrapers, rockets, and innumerable products to use however we see fit. We have also made tremendous advancements in getting back in touch with our souls. We know we are energy and live in a universe of energy.

American theoretical physicist David Bohm suggested the Universe has both an explicate and an implicate order. His model claims that the entire Universe and every particle in it includes an explicate order resulting from active information held energetically in an underlying implicate order. His theory explains everything that exists holds the information of everything else. We hold energetically the knowledge of the entire universe in every single cell. That means our spiritual self has an implicit knowledge of everything in the universe. It does not imply an understanding of everything. As spiritual creatures, we tend to want to experiment with everything that comes into our field of consciousness. Our souls continually form, reform, change, manifest our futures, and experience thought. Our souls also experience everything we experience throughout life.

Our souls are continually forming, thinking, creating our futures, and reforming themselves at conception. Just as our body replaces cells every seven years, so does our soul. Our thoughts originate in our souls, and our memories are in our souls. It took us millions of years to develop into human beings during our lives on earth. We evolved from tiny creatures to the size we are today, and it appears that future humans will attain larger frames than they have today. We, as souls, enjoy our presence on earth as we continue to multiply. Few animals reproduce asexually, but 99 percent of them, including humans, require a male and a female to produce more animals. We use sex to reproduce because it can be fun and feels good for both parties. Many humans try to replicate themselves asexually, but so far, with no luck. The female always has the egg, and the male fertilizes the egg to create new humans. Parts of the female and male souls enter the newly forming human at conception. The memories of both parents, some of their forebears, and spiritual memories in the atmosphere add to the new soul that isn't new. The memory of one parent may be more potent and dominate the memories of the soon-to-be-delivered child. The memories may also become garbled or disappear by being overridden during their time in purely spiritual existence. It isn't that a new soul forms, but two existing souls pass along energy to combine and create a new body for their combined spiritual energy to use.

There is confusion as to the soul's location in the body. Many spiritual people believe we find it throughout the body, and it stretches to the end of the aura, extending outward up to 15 or 20 feet and possibly further. Other people believe it is in the brain, while others believe it is somewhere in the head, the heart, or the whole body. There is no scientific proof yet, but the soul has to disassociate itself from Universal Energy somewhere, and the end of the aura is one logical place. The soul is you. If you can feel your aura, you can feel your soul. Empaths are susceptible to their feelings and the feelings of others, and they can pick up feelings from people a great distance from themselves. Picking up feelings of love is much healthier than picking up unhappy, angry feelings.

THOUGHTS

- Everything in the Universe is energy
- Everything in the Universe is from the same Energy
- People differ because their energy vibrates at different levels
- Empaths are susceptible to the Energy of others
- Human beings have unlimited potential
- Abuse interferes with communication
- It is possible to change energy, but it cannot be created or destroyed
- There are over 1 trillion species currently on Earth
- It took us millions of years to develop as humans

CHAPTER 12
LOVE IS IMPORTANT

YOU WOULD BELIEVE SPIRITUAL PEOPLE ARE FULL OF LOVE and tenderness for their fellow human beings, but that doesn't seem to be the case throughout the earth's history. We have already gone over the history of our physical development. There has not been a time filled with peace and love since the birth of the earth. We are the energy of God, the Universe, or pure energy. We are spirits. When people speak about our afterlife or even spirits not in human form, they tell us how smart and wonderful they are. To a lesser extent, they also talk about evil spirits, but only in guarding against them and protecting themselves or others from them. Some people enjoy watching movies about evil spirits, and children often enjoy ghost stories.

When you understand we are spiritual energy, you don't have to separate yourself from what we call ghosts, goblins, and creatures that go bump in the night. They are us, and we are them. When you look out into space, you will see confusion, disarray, and turbulence throughout the Universe. Worlds run into each other, stars get old and burn out, and areas of the Universe seem peaceful. As human beings, we also experience calmness and confusion. We grow old, get burned out, and become angry at times. We behave exactly like spiritual entities, such as angels, apparitions, and the Universe as a whole. One part of your body can hurt, like a sore knee, and the rest can feel okay. Say you hit your thumb with a hammer when you are nailing a picture on the wall. That thumb is going to hurt. You might jump around and even stick the thumb into your mouth to soothe it. But your other thumb and the rest of your body are fine. As energy beings, we act like all the other energy in the universe. One aspect of the Universe, such as the sun, can explode, and the rest of the Universe will still flourish and keep growing and changing. We are microcosms of the macrocosm.

For at least two 2,000 years, we have said we should love our neighbor as ourselves, but it hasn't worked. We have all kinds of definitions of love, but people use them to describe whatever they want it to be. Some dictionary definitions of love describe it as an intense feeling of affection, a great interest in something, an attraction based on sexual desire, or appreciation for something. When people join as a couple, they usually tell each other they love each other no matter how they feel. Often, it is merely an association of convenience. When speaking of spiritual love because we are spirits, the one aspect that is little understood is you cannot love another person more than you love yourself. Narcissists will tell you they love you while they continually abuse you. They call it love, but it isn't love. It is abuse. Narcissists do not even like themselves. They get a feeling of power when they control other people's actions.

People call it love when they develop a sexual relationship. Although it can be wonderful when you experience a sexual relationship with someone you love, they are two different things. Spiritually, when you love someone, you always want what is best for them. They will respect any boundaries you have set for yourself. You will appreciate their limits. Often, we will hear someone make excuses for the treatment they receive from their lover who mistreats them. That is not love. That is more akin to slavery. Years ago, I had a friend who wanted to find a man to marry her. She said any man would do. I asked her if she would marry him if he beat her. Much to my surprise, she said she would put up with it. Since then, I have interviewed men who felt the same way. They just needed a companion. Whatever the relationship was like, they would call it love.

Spiritual people aren't any better or worse than other people are. But spiritual people can and will change the world into a better, more pleasant place because most want honest love, harmony, and joy. They recognize that what they experience on Earth is a precursor to their future existence. Spiritual people, who recognize their life on earth is just one stop on their journey through eternity, can establish guidelines to follow to help themselves bring peace and happiness to the world.

The history of peace and happiness is one of somebody preaching about peace, love, and joy. Everybody agrees it is a good idea. Then, bad guys step in and want to have power over everybody else. The good guys accommodate the bad guys and compromise with them. Everyone is happy for a while. Then, the bad guys want more power or control, and possibly the good guys give in a little more. This activity keeps repeating until the good guys finally get so exasperated, they fight back. A fight or a war breaks out, and the good guys act just like the bad guys and destroy, or get destroyed, by them. Whoever wins the ultimate battle, the balance between the good and bad starts all over again. Throughout history, evil angels, spirits, people, or whatever you want to call them, have played a significant role in the emotional atmosphere of the world. Over the past 5,000 years, the good guys have slowly nudged the world into being more peaceful and loving.

Several years ago, America was suffering from a very divided government. The economy was doing poorly, crime was up, taxes from the government were stifling people, its borders were unprotected, and other countries were threatening to remove America from its position as the leader of the free world. Since its beginning, America has been a magnet for people disenchanted with their own country. Its freedoms, such as freedom of speech, freedom of movement, and the right to self-defense, promised them they could have a good life. Over the years, America thrived. As America grew and prospered, it developed a political class that lived off of the sweat of ordinary people. The country grew so wealthy it started losing the memory of what brought it to so much wealth and power. A very wealthy man felt the government had gotten too large and overbearing, so he ran for president and won. Before he ran, he was famous and had many wealthy friends in the two largest popular political parties. The moment he announced he would run for president, the people in the party he didn't represent turned on him. Also, many of the people in his party turned on him because they were comfortable with the all-powerful, overloaded government.

He suddenly became a liar and thief, meaner than a junkyard dog, a womanizer, stupid, and just out to make more money. They said he wasn't knowledgeable, didn't know how to run a business, and would quickly get America into a war. He was so bad that he would absolutely ruin America. He won the election despite the political insiders being against him and abetted by the mainstream media. During his four-year term, he kept America out of foreign wars, helped the economy, lowered the national crime rate, and put the country back on the road to prosperity. He is no better or worse than any other soul. He is a spirit walking around in human flesh like the rest of us. He just knew how to run a business very well. But the people who would profit most from his success ganged him up on. They didn't see it that way, and during his four years in office, not a day went by that they didn't accuse him of something terrible. They tried to throw him out of the office twice without success. After his term was over and he was out of office, one thing they accused him of doing, getting another country to help him, was proven to be done to him by them. They tried to get the other country to help them against him.

He served for four years and ran for reelection against a person who made minimal effort to campaign against him. Surprisingly, the other person won more votes than anyone had ever received before that election. The ex-president claimed they rigged the election, but up to this time could not prove it. The political elite continued to work at disqualifying him from ever running for election again. The hate by the entrenched politicians and media continued just as vehemently as it was when he was in office. They did not want him to run again, but many of the states where he had lost changed the rules of their elections to ensure there would be no cheating in future elections. The fight between him and the government hierarchy is like the fight that has been going on for centuries. It is a fight between the people in power and those not in power who want to be in control.

After the fighting, one side will come out on top and set the agenda for politics in America in the future. The country will settle down, people will prosper and work together for a while, or there will be a period of disharmony. Change is how the Universe works. It expands and contracts. There are places in the Universe filled with love and areas filled with hate. The Universe is like all the matter, spirits, and animals it created: ever-changing, ever-vibrating.

On Earth, the present time is one of massive upheaval. People who feared their leaders in the past no longer have this fear. Wars don't seem to last as long and be as destructive. Although if one crazy dictator with a bunch of nuclear bombs decides to blow up the world, the possibility of the earth becoming an uninhabitable planet for a thousand years is a possibility. People all over the world are developing a taste for freedom and happiness. We have come a long way in feeding and caring for people in order to keep everyone well. We now have the means to provide for everyone who wants to live in paradise. Happiness and love are much more attractive and enjoyable than anger and hate. As more and more people understand this, they will infect the haters and abusers. It will happen slowly, but it will happen.

The understanding that we, as human beings, are spiritual souls spending time on Earth is spreading quickly. Also, the awareness we are responsible for our own happiness is quickly spreading. We no longer depend on the state to tell us what we must do, how we must behave, or anything. We can be happy and loving and live in harmony with whoever we choose. We will be at the forefront of change for the earth to be like a heaven. We will always have changing feelings and emotions because that is how the Universe works. Everything in the Universe is constantly changing. But everything we do affects the Universe and especially the people near us. The idea, as spirits, is to maintain our feelings of love, joy, and harmony in varying degrees. Anger and unhappiness will enter our lives, but as we learn to understand our emotions better, we will learn to adjust them positively. We have to learn a few easy-to-do things that will enable us to maintain a loving and happy equilibrium.

Meditation improves our spiritual essence, which will help us influence those around us to live better lives. The first thing meditation does for us is to teach us how to focus our thoughts. The better we can focus our thoughts, the better we keep our equilibrium joyfully and lovingly. Meditation helps us overcome stress so we can relax and withstand the criticism and attacks of disruptive people. It also helps us overcome anxiety when we face unpleasant situations. We must stick to our truth and practice it in every case to improve the world. When we show our fear or timidity, unhappy or disturbed individuals will attempt to take advantage of us. The troubled, disgruntled, and perverse people of the world have taken advantage of the kinder people for centuries. We, as spiritual people, are now standing up to them.

Meditating helps us develop a strong self-awareness; it helps us know who we are and what we stand for. Our individuality shows when we meditate and gain the inner strength to express our views about living with love, joy, and harmony. We also set boundaries for ourselves that we refuse to allow others to cross. Giving in to aggressive, unhappy people has kept the world in turmoil since the beginning of recorded history. We, as spiritual people, just by our presence, will change that. Along with our use of meditation, we need to teach the truth about love and the individual right of each of us to love more than one person. We must teach the benefits of forgiving those who wrong us and our responsibility for creating our happiness.

Learn to Love and Feel Happiness while on Earth

We don't need to go to war or organize a movement to change the world into a paradise; we need to be honest. We need to stand up for what we believe in, and we need to treat our adversaries with polite respect. We also need to tell them to listen to us and treat us with polite respect. We need to use our ability to be calm and smile in a friendly manner. In the past, one or two people have spoken out, such as Jesus Christ, and he was crucified. The world has made enough progress in the last 2,000 years that they no longer crucify people. In some countries, you are still liable to get killed or thrown in jail if you say something the government disapproves of, but that is less and less. The governments of many countries now allow their people to protest and complain about their policies. The freedom for people to complain about their government will slowly continue to improve. There will continue to be a few rogue nations, but they will become less powerful and fewer and fewer in the future. Happiness, freedom, and joy are so much more powerful than hate and meanness that things will naturally get better with or without the help of governments. But as more and more people understand we are souls living as humans, the impetus to improve life right now increases.

People unknowingly pick up the traits of other people with whom they associate. You pick up the characteristics of the people with whom you associate. The people who associate with you unconsciously pick up your traits. When we mindlessly react in the accustomed way and get accepted by those we associate with, we improve or change very little. We pass on more of the same old poor emotions. You can be the one who starts an improvement in yourself and everyone with whom you associate.

First, you must forgive yourself for everything you did wrong, mean, and evil. You may have aborted babies, kicked little old ladies, abused your siblings, and stolen from your own family. Think of every mean, cruel, horrible thing you ever did in this lifetime. Do your shadow work. As spiritual people, we must encourage our friends to do their shadow work. Shadow work is like confessing our lousy or possibly criminal behavior to someone close to us or ourselves. We must make amends for what we perceive as we have done wrong in our lives.

Now, understand you have been going through different phases of life since the beginning of time. Also, realize everybody you have ever loved, tolerated, hated, or abused has been around since the beginning. We are all spiritual and easily influenced by the energy that surrounds us. Yes, you have made horrible mistakes, but everyone has made awful mistakes. Our time on Earth is to correct our mistaken behaviors and set a good example for ourselves and others. We do that when we can make our every act one that comes from our ability to act with love from the depth of our soul. We can turn our time on Earth into a time of paradise. It can become a wonderful time of love, joy, and harmony when we truly act as our spiritual selves; our souls vibrate the way they do when they experience pure passion, fun, peace, and fellowship.

It can be fearful for you to act with love and harmony with other people. Last week, I went to a doctor's appointment. Nothing important, just an annual visit where the doctor would tell me I was still alive and healthy. This lady doctor looked me over and acted like I was the most important person in the world to her. She probably forgot all about me the second the examination was over, but she made me feel special. I was important to her when she observed me to see if anything was wrong with me. When she was satisfied I would live for a while longer, she had no reason to spend more time thinking about me. For all I know, she spent time with her next patient and treated them just as well as she treated me. I didn't spend more time thinking about her because I had other places to go, and new thoughts were entering my mind. It will be wonderful when our every encounter can be as pleasant as this one was.

Our souls constantly produce new thoughts for us to consider. She had other patients for which she needed to care. But I certainly appreciated her interest in me for the short period she saw me. Happy, warm, and satisfied is how people typically feel when others pay proper attention to them. All we have to do is to be respectful to others, listen to them, and be truthful to them, to teach them how to treat others. You can start a chain reaction to spread the idea that treating others lovingly and courteously is good. Even the worst of your relatives will get the idea when you treat them well while refusing to allow them to cross your boundaries. Respect yourself for the eternal, spiritual entity you are.

Most people do not even know what love is. They never think about it or even attempt to define it. If you are nice to them and believe they can get something from you, they will tell you they love you. They know the words "I love you" are enough to make most people believe they love them, so they think you will give them whatever they want. You can love anyone, and it is a good idea to love everybody, even those you don't appreciate. But you build self-confidence, self-esteem, and independence when focusing on self-love rather than getting others to love you. You can form healthier and happier relationships, not only with yourself, but with others.

Many people seem to love others more than they love themselves. It is as if someone taught them it is wrong to love yourself. Many parents tell their children they are evil and had better change their ways, or they will go to hell or some such place. Some churches teach we are born in sin and must spend our lives getting rid of that sin. Many people have a powerful and very influential inner critic. We get into unhealthy relationships, take drugs, and abuse alcohol. We hide our honesty, act like others want us to, and, as a result, treat ourselves poorly. Many of us do our best to look good to others rather than show our honest selves. It is time to love ourselves with at least the same amount of love we show others. When you do this, you'll find you treat people better than you did before. You will also find many people will return your good will toward them.

Self-love is not selfish. It improves your relationship with yourself and shows other people how to love you. You always have to live with yourself. You must like yourself, enjoy your company, recognize your good qualities, and take care of yourself. Besides getting rid of anger and learning to love and practicing love, we can develop the quality of spiritual wisdom while spending our time on earth. Our love, joy, and harmony will be contagious. The more we experience it on earth, the more likely we will carry it with us during our next incarnation, wherever and whenever it is. We will enter different dimensions on and off during our time in eternity. Preparing to withstand the vagaries of whatever we will face in the next go-round is wise. The odds are very good for us if we can create an atmosphere of love, kindness, understanding, and harmony in this life to carry over into our next life. One particular type of soul we describe as an empath needs to work on developing and sticking to powerful boundaries. Many empaths exhibit strong spiritual qualities before they even realize they are empaths. Love is powerful.

THOUGHTS

- Human thoughts are just like spiritual thoughts
- You want what is best for the people you love
- Love and sex are two different things
- Many people will marry anyone who will have them
- The world is slowly becoming more peaceful
- Confused spirits often thwart the desires of peaceful spirits
- Love and joy are more powerful than hate
- Your soul helps you better when you are relaxed
- It is not selfish to love yourself

CHAPTER 13
EMPATHY AND EMPATHS

ARE YOU AN EMPATHETIC PERSON? IF YOU ARE, YOU CAN feel proud about it. People with a strong sense of empathy often take the spiritual path. Science often obfuscates whether actual empathetic people, or empaths, really exist. Millions of people claim to have the quality. Dictionaries claim it is simply the ability to feel other people's emotions. It is also the ability to recognize, adopt, understand, and share the thoughts of other people, animals, or even fictional characters. It's the activity of understanding, being aware of, and being sensitive to the feelings, thoughts, and experiences of others. Empathy is crucial for establishing warm relationships with others and behaving compassionately. For spiritual people, the trait is common. When we transcend to our next period after this one, empaths customarily want to go to a place filled with love and happiness. This desire differs from the religious people who plan to go to heaven. Religious people have an ultimate place, like heaven, while spiritual people generally see life as a continuum with many places to go.

The spiritual person usually expects to continue the journey to another dimension, another life on Earth, or somewhere else in the Universe. A significant difference between religious and spiritual people is that spiritual people often believe we are living souls wearing bodies during our time on Earth, while religious people feel we are physical creatures with souls. While living on Earth, it is a beautiful time for spiritual people to prepare for their next period of existence.

For religious people, it appears to be their last chance to experience life as a physical being. Those who believe they will have an afterlife want to experience happiness in it. If so, they must understand what happiness is for themselves and how they have it. Happiness means different things to different people. Generally, a cheerful person feels pleasure, satisfaction, cheerfulness, glee, delight, or many other positive emotions. They experience nothing like hate, regret, or depression. Happiness is everything good.

Most spiritual people believe that when we transgress, we continue experiencing a similar type of reality we have as humans. It is beneficial for spiritual people, who are empathetic to the feelings of others, to learn how to keep their happy realities through whatever they experience. Being an empath can be a burden. Until they learn to take control of their emotions, other people can control them through their words and actions. They often will act how people around them perceive them. People who perceive them as mean or cruel will probably receive meanness or cruelty from them. These same emotions can also give them a greater understanding of the vagaries of life. As they become comfortable with their feelings of empathy and understand them, they learn to resist the control of others. They often become very understanding and patient with the confusing behavior of others.

Empaths are susceptible to the thoughts of others and easily connect with people. They are good listeners and deeply see and feel the truth in any situation. They see the world more deeply than other people. Empaths can read others without obvious cues and sense the truth about what's beneath the surface without being told. They instinctively know if someone is lying to them. The more empathetic they are, the more their knowing and psychic ability becomes substantial.

The empath's ability to listen through all their senses gives people communicating with them the idea they are being heard and understood. They can become so immersed in conversations with others that the other person will tell them their life story. They will always react to the problems of others to help them, even if it risks their ongoing relationships. Shopping malls, stadiums, big box stores, and supermarkets where masses of people gather can be pleasurable to them. Still, when the crowds are large, it can become overwhelming and even lead to nervousness, or even panic attacks, because of the myriad of emotions they sense. They often steer clear of being around large groups of people.

Empaths are probably best known for their ability to take on the emotions of others. It is common for them to take on the feelings of others and not even realize what they are doing. They mirror the feelings of others and take them on as if they were their own. At times, it can make it very difficult for them to distinguish what belongs to themself or someone else, and life can become overwhelming. Developing a solid self-awareness gives the empath greater control over their emotions and the ability to determine whose emotions they feel and not get caught up in them.

Empaths are likely to experience extreme emotional highs and lows, making their behavior unpredictable sometimes. Physically, they are in tune with their soul, which controls their feelings. One minute they can feel happy and the next minute feel low. These highs and lows often result from what they pick up from others. This emotional instability can be confusing and depressing. They can demand attention. If they feel someone doesn't treat them right, they may come across as needy, even selfish. Although a narcissist might abuse them, once they realize they are used by anyone, they do their best to stop it. They toughen up and grow spiritually stronger.

You are likely to be an empath if you get upset when you see someone harmed in real life or in a movie. Shocking scenes of cruelty or physical pain can bring an empath to tears. Empaths are likely to feel any pain shown by others. It is their natural response, and they will do almost anything to ease it. The pain and illness they see in others becomes their pain, and they can sometimes feel it as deeply as the other person experiences it.

Empaths typically have a certain charisma that draws people to them. This charisma subconsciously scares many of them, and they gain weight or subconsciously try to make themselves unattractive to keep people away from them. But they will still draw people who see something in them they want. Strangers will occasionally approach them and quickly act like they are best friends. This quick attachment will often feel very good to the empath, but other times, it will scare the heebie-jeebies out of them. People quickly develop an innate trust and feel relaxed and comfortable in the presence of most empaths.

It is usual for empaths to want to help people. Many of them enter the helping professions, such as social work or some kind of medical practice. They are drawn to helping others and often take on more than their fair share when working with people. Their work with others frequently wears them down and causes fatigue, which is difficult for them to overcome. Often, they need daily naps or work breaks to replenish their energy. It is common for them to become involved in healing, holistic health, or caring activities. A career as a doctor, nurse, social worker, psychologist, naturopath, or veterinarian often draws empaths. They will usually have pets, especially if they are single adults. They love to give and receive unconditional love from dogs, cats, rabbits, and all living creatures. And they are often advocates or supporters of the prevention of cruelty to animals. They enjoy being outdoors, in the forest or high mountains, and connecting with the land. They often want to escape from the busy world to rejuvenate their senses. They need someone or something to share their love with, and they can be very loving. They make wonderful mates. They can get so involved with who or what they work with that they get worn out. They must learn to recognize other people's effects on them so they can step aside for short periods to recuperate their energy.

Empaths Are Unique

Empaths have a natural curiosity and continually search for truth in their life. They question most of what they learn until it feels honest and accurate. Their curiosity is lifelong, but occasionally quelled by their friends' and relatives' criticism or taunting. However, their curiosity will always strive to reawaken, which will happen if given a chance. Their curiosity often leads them to explore the spiritual side of life, as they tend to have a deep sense of spirituality. They won't necessarily be religious, but will explore many facets of religion and spirituality to satisfy their spiritual urges. The occult often draws their interest, but only as a source of information on their search for oneness with a source of energy most people call God.

Empathetic people usually have close relatives with similar traits. Spiritual people with similar thoughts, beliefs, and feelings attract them. When they are very young, they love listening to stories of olden times and their ancestors. From a young age, they are the children who listen to the stories of old that get passed down throughout the generations. They are genuinely interested in knowing where they came from, who their ancestors were, and what they did in their lifetime. While young, they may have memories of past lives, but these memories have faded mainly by the time they reach their teenage years. As they grow older, they will probably record the family tree and collect photographs of the various living family members. It is important for them to connect with their siblings and children.

They tend to be quiet achievers who prefer to do the hard work behind the scenes, but you often find them in leadership positions because of their ability to be focused. They are more comfortable praising others rather than accepting praises and often meditate to maintain a balance of harmony. Living a quiet life is enticing for them. Although they can be and often are friendly, they are content with their own company. They enjoy the tranquility that can come from living in a quiet place or alone. Relaxing while reading a book, drawing a picture, or pursuing a hobby is a beautiful experience for them. While pursuing their interests, they will often find themselves distracted, their minds will wander off, and they will experience creative daydreams about almost anything filled with love and joy.

They have a deep desire to experience harmony in everything they do. They crave mental stimulation, and a well-developed empath can focus intensely on one project at a time, whether at school, work, play, or simply around their house. If a project bores them, they wander into their joyful dreamland. They are unique and loveable. They have a deep desire to explore life, usually through their love of reading about it, and will seek information about travel to far-off places and enjoyable activities nearby. They are free-spirited and love to escape the normal constraints of the world, if only in their minds. If they don't have the opportunity to do this as often as they like, they can become agitated.

Most empaths love the healing qualities of water. Whether soaking in the tub, swimming in the sea, paddling around in a swimming pool, or even walking in the rain, empaths sense the healing power of water. They have no problems drinking enough water daily to keep themselves healthy. They enjoy liquid refreshments so much they occasionally drink too many sugared or spirited refreshments that are not good for their health. They sense a spiritual connection with their souls and physical bodies through the water.

Since the early formation of life on Earth, empathy has led the way to the creation of love, happiness, harmony, and every type of healthy advancement achieved. Empaths do whatever they can to experience peace and love. They constantly work to make things right when they perceive they are wrong. They have a sense of how to make energy flow in their environment with joyful peace and harmony. When society tells them they are wrong, they continue to practice their beliefs and have a powerful effect on others. Through the years, they have released the energy that has caused the entire world to become a safer and more hospitable place to live. They are now engaged in a terrific battle with spiritual demons to control whether this world will become a paradise or hell for the next thousand years. The empaths will eventually win because love and joy are much more powerful than anger and hate.

Empaths wholeheartedly dive into any project they start. When they start a project, they do it intending to put forth their best effort, and they usually do. The downside is that the people they work with don't always put forth the same effort, and the empath wears out and needs time to recuperate. When they recover, they dig in just as vehemently as they did before, but after it happens several times, their interests will turn elsewhere. They don't do anything halfway. It is all or nothing, and they often get disappointed because their fellow workers don't put the same amount of energy into projects as they do.

They do not appreciate conflict. It is highly unsettling to them, whether with friends, families, or strangers. Historically, they have always tried to mediate disputes. Now, they express their honest feelings more and more while advocating for peace, love, and joy. They say their opinions about the best solutions and then go their way whether or not others agree with them. They have a subconscious understanding that their actions can influence the behavior of those they interact with. They also appreciate that other people will adapt to the rightness of their ways.

They are sensitive to antiques and old objects. When they enter old buildings, touch old things, or handle anything that has aged, they often get vivid and accurate information about the past owner's history and life experiences. They are natural psychic readers. This sensitivity can be highly problematic to empaths who do not understand what is happening. It can cause them to feel like they are thinking thoughts they should not be thinking or just nervous because they think they shouldn't have the ideas they have. Those aware of their sensitivity, who understand it, feel perfectly comfortable with the sensations they receive. Empaths dream. And they have vivid dreams. They often enjoy their dreams because they are usually about their future and what they want to accomplish. They also sometimes dream about experiences in their past. They can often determine their role in their dreams and use them as rehearsals for future activities. They often have vivid dreams starting at a very young age, while they can control aspects of them with willful thought alone. They believe their dreams directly relate to their awake state and use them to find answers that guide them with wisdom.

Dr. Michael Banissy, one of the many people who studied traits or qualities of an empath, said, "That while many people claim to be empaths, they may just feel empathy at a higher level or are hypersensitive." Dr. Banissy lists a bunch of ways a person can be an empath, and there are many levels of them, and possibly the more ways you are sensitive, the more empathetic you would be. The highest level would perhaps be loving angels, and the lowest level would be someone with totally no empathy.

There are all kinds of empaths. Among them are familial empaths, such as mothers who have a very close bond with their children and often know when their children are in pain or need help. They may not get these feelings for anyone else, but they get them for one or more of their children. Also, siblings and twins sometimes empathize with their brothers and sisters. Physical empaths also feel other people's physical conditions as if they were their own. They will react similarly when watching a movie or hearing a story. They develop the same feelings of pain and discomfort. But it will uplift them when they are around someone happy or feeling exceptionally well.

As empaths are emotional, there is a type called emotional empaths. They feel the emotions of others. This emotional contagion is common, as even narcissists often pick up on people's feelings. It is great when you are an emotional empath and your friend is feeling good, but your emotions will probably go down to the same level when they feel down. One challenge of empaths is to see what is happening, step back from the situation, and observe it rather than experience it. Emotional empaths can become exhausted by complainers who focus on the negative or narcissists who take all the attention and never reciprocate when the empath feels down. Emotional empaths are emotional sponges. They become emotionally drained by psychic vampires and energy thieves. By practicing self-care and learning how to differentiate other people's emotions from your own, you can master this gift.

An intuitive empath knows if and what needs doing in a situation without solid evidence or rationalization. Intuitive empaths know whether they should do something, depending on the context and circumstances of the case. They feel the energy field of others and can scan people quickly. Intuitive empaths generally sense the unspoken in terms of what's going on. Telepathic empaths use a form of telepathy to sense the thoughts and the emotions of others. Psychic readers often have this capacity. As people's beliefs influence their feelings, and their emotions affect their thoughts, an empath's power may allow them to read minds, acting as a mixture of empathy and telepathy. There are nature empaths who connect with the Earth and all vegetation. They do a fantastic job of growing flowers, shrubs, and trees. They seem always to know how to treat anything growing in ways that allow it to flourish. They tune into the vibrations of vegetation. They are also sensitive to changes in weather and disruptions to the Earth.

Animal empaths have unique relationships with animals. Animals quickly recognize they will care for them and not harm them. They have a special connection with animals and can usually feel their needs and communicate with them lovingly and relaxedly. They almost always have at least one pet and, often, have several of them. They hate to see any violence directed at any animal. Some animal empaths seem to prefer the company of animals over people.

A psychometric empath can feel information from inanimate objects, such as old homes, photographs, and famous landmarks. Psychic empaths often act as mediums or psychic readers. They pick up information on people in their presence, and when they hold on to others, they receive powerful impressions about what is occurring in their life. They pick up impressions that can help them guide others through their times of turmoil.

Heyoka empaths are said to be a special type of empath. Everyone is said to be empathic sometimes, but Heyokas are always that way.

They are considered excellent friends, advisors, and partners because of their mighty empathetic powers. They mirror other people's emotions and make them aware of how they are acting. It is said that they prefer to be alone, but they also have strong social skills, although their sometimes blunt truth-telling can cause people to become uncomfortable. It is said that the Heyoka empaths are profoundly spiritual and have a strong connection with their soul and universal energy.

Anyone reading this book probably has the features of an empath. Some of the main ones are that you are sensitive and pick up on what is happening around you. You may get your feelings hurt relatively quickly, but you want to help and live in harmony with others. If you have never set boundaries for how you allow people to treat you, you need to, because it will save you from a world of hurt. You also may be an ambivert, welcoming people you appreciate and trust, and avoiding those you don't trust or respect. Empathy is a characteristic some humans have had since we began populating the Earth as much as 6 million years ago. In the beginning, the struggle for survival and healing their physical bodies took all their energy. We've come to a time where there is very little new in their healing or survival needs.

THOUGHTS

- Empathy is a common trait of spiritual people
- Happiness means different things to different people
- Happy people feel pleasure, cheerfulness, and delight
- Empaths can be susceptible to the thoughts of others
- Empaths need to set boundaries for themselves
- Empaths need to abide by their boundaries
- Empaths take on the emotions of others
- There are all kinds of empaths
- You very likely are empathetic

CHAPTER 14
SPIRITUAL HEALING

MOST PEOPLE BELIEVE IN A GOD. SOME IMAGINE GOD TO be a large man who knows everything we do, a person who watches over us, judges us, or another powerful force that controls everything. At least one God decides whether we go to heaven, hell, purgatory, or another place when we leave this life on Earth. Most people also believe in spiritual or invisible power, whether it be the breath of life, Qui, auras, or an evil energy no one understands. They feel there is an invisible force which we can use to heal those in need of a cure for their illness. This belief dates back as far as anyone remembers, and it comes with the belief of our spiritual history. There are stories that before there was an earth, everyone lived in heaven as angels. Then, the angel Lucifer, who turned into Satan, or had a lieutenant called Satan, started a rebellion. So, God threw the rebellious angels out and down to hell, which was in the center of the earth. There are similar stories, but they all say approximately the same thing as this one. Then God supposedly created the earth and Adam and Eve, who evidently arrived on Earth as fully grown adults. He also placed them in the beautiful Garden of Eden with gob loads of food. Like the angels, they quickly disobeyed him, too. So, he kicked them out of the garden. From then on, they and their ancestors had to work to survive during their time on Earth. All of this led them to believe that if they treated God right, he would help them when they needed it if they cooperated with him. They understood the idea of spiritual energy.

About 2,500 years ago, a Greek citizen named Plato said he believed knowledge was the primary energy of the universe. Since then, many people felt Plato got it right. There are several theories about what the basis of the Universe is. Some physicists say it's subatomic particles, while others believe it's energy or space-time. One of the latest and more radical theories, which has a powerful chance to be right, suggests that information is the fundamental element of the cosmos. In the mid-20th century, Claude Elwood Shannon developed the classical information theory. Scientists do not universally accept this theory, but it claims that every aspect of a particle is expressed as information. Subatomic particles we call spiritual energy particles may be the bits the universe is processing like a giant supercomputer. It isn't often mentioned, but these particles supply the energy which heals or damages us.

John Wheeler of the University of Texas said the Universe has three parts. First, "Everything is particles," second, "Everything is fields," and third, "Everything is information." Several years ago, a team of physicists concluded we might live in a giant hologram. It is important to note that most physicists believe energy is the fundamental or essential unit of the Universe. Spiritual people describe the total fundamental energy as spiritual energy. Wheeler felt the Universe is participatory, where consciousness holds a central role. Other scientists argue the cosmos has specific properties which allow it to create and sustain life. Most spiritual people believe life is spiritual energy existing as humanity, worlds, animals, and everything else. The idea that the cosmos sustains life agrees with most people's thinking. If the cosmos didn't sustain life, we wouldn't be here today.

Earth, the planet of our current residence, formed about 4.5 billion years ago when gravity pulled swirling dust and gas together to become a spinning planet circling the sun. Like other terrestrial planets, Earth has a central core, a rocky mantle, and a solid crust. It has only been called Earth for about 1,000 years. The earliest life forms we know of were microscopic organisms (microbes) that left signals of their presence in rocks about 3.7 billion years ago. The signals comprised a type of carbon molecule produced by living things. These organisms gradually formed clusters of cells, which may have helped them to feed more efficiently or gain protection from unknown sources by becoming larger. Living collectively, each cell, as spiritual energy does, soon supported the group's needs by doing a specific job. Some cells made junctions to hold the group together. Others made digestive enzymes that could break down food, and others worked on their evolution to grow bigger and stronger. Could you see yourself as a spiritually conscious spiritual dweller of the swamp? That's about what we were. We were still thought creatures or angel dwellers of the swamp.

These clusters of specialized, cooperating cells eventually became the first animals, which DNA evidence suggests evolved around 800 million years ago. Sponges were among the earliest animals. While chemical compounds from sponges show up in rocks as old as 700 million years, molecular evidence points to sponges developing even earlier. The first mammals are said to have appeared in the Late Triassic epoch about 225 million years ago, 40 million years after the first therapsids. They were tiny reptilian creatures. Our first human ancestors appeared between 5 million and 7 million years ago, probably when apelike animals lived in trees and walked on two legs. They were using crude, homemade tools about 2.5 million years ago. Bones of primitive Homo sapiens first appeared 300,000 years ago in Africa, with brains as large or larger than ours. They were followed by anatomically modern Homo sapiens at least 200,000 years ago, and our brain shape became essentially modern at least 100,000 years ago. At that time, humans spread all over the planet, continuing to evolve into the size and structure we are now. One significant change was the brain developing areas to store memory fed from our minds.

Spiritual energy continually changes and evolves. Change and evolvement can be for its benefit or for depredation. Evolution is a gradual, peaceful, progressive change or development. You, as a spiritual entity, continually evolve. An example is an 80-year-old woman who differs from what she was at four years old. This evolution enables you to program yourself for how you manage the challenges that enter your life. Understanding and using the ability to control one's evolution is a beautiful aspect of leading life as a spiritual being.

Mary Myers grew up in a fundamental churchgoing family. As a child, she learned we are born to suffer for the sins of man and that we must constantly repent for our sins. As an adult, Mary continued to pray for years. When she was 31, she met her husband, Cory. When she told Cory about praying while they were dating, he laughed and asked her why she prayed so much. This original prayer discussion led to other intense conversations about spirituality and religion. Cory told her he believed we were all angels wearing bodies and that his God allowed each angel to decide whether it wanted to thrive or suffer. He explained to her that good people go to a good place when they die, and bad people go to a terrible place because they carry their human traits along with them.

Mary had heard nothing like what Cory said, and although it differed from anything she believed, she became intrigued by his words. He explained how he felt we live in a spiritual universe, and we are all formed from its energy. He explained how energy and matter are the same but have different consistencies. Our bodies have both types of energy, he told her. The idea we are angels carrying around bodies caught her attention. She had always thought that we were caretakers for a soul that she had to take care of, and she had to be good and pray to keep God happy so her soul could go to heaven when she died. She immediately understood what he told her, but it went against everything she knew. It took her about a month to fully grasp and accept it as the truth. Now they meditate together and heal each other spiritually when they are sick or unhappy.

Hospitals Now Use Healing Touch

As spiritual beings, we need to keep our bodies healthy while on earth. We use them until it is time for us to transcend to another dimension. Many spiritual people meditate daily to help themselves focus and bring themselves into balance with their God or the Universe. They also do spiritual healing to help themselves reconnect with the wise, loving, powerful, creative being they are at their core. There are many types of spiritual healing. Among them are aura healing or reiki, physical healing, mental healing, emotional healing, holistic healing, and subtle healing.

Some spiritual healers focus on bringing balance to the body's etheric or non-physical energy field. Many Shamanic healers concentrate on restoring the spirit and curing the loss of soul material. Other spiritual healers focus on unifying the body, heart, mind, and spirit. Even psychologists and therapists are using forms of spiritual healing.

Jerri Ferguson's child, Stevie, was 16 months old when he developed a breathing problem. He gagged for air incessantly and had trouble holding down his food. There was a problem with his lymphatic system. He was in the hospital hooked up to machines to help him breathe, and after two days of constant crying, the nurse suggested to Jerri they try healing touch on the poor child. She explained to Jerri that it's a therapy to help the body heal through near-body contact or physical touch. Jerri didn't have anything to lose and was ready to try anything, so she told her to go ahead. Jerri sat in a recliner with her son in her arms. She watched as the nurse slowly moved her hands slightly above the heads of her and her child. Within minutes, the machines hooked up to her child stopped beeping, and he quit crying. Soon he was sound asleep. During the healing session, the nurse's hands never touched the child. Jerri said she felt both confused and relieved.

Healing touch is based on the idea that near body or light touch can support the body's healing ability. While medical practices like healing touch are on the fringe of standard medical practice, the Mayo Clinic, Memorial Sloan Kettering Cancer Center, and over 30 percent of America's Veteran's Hospitals use it to comfort patients. Scientists can't fully explain why the practice works, but some controlled studies have guessed that something profound happens below the surface.

Aura healing and laying on hands have been with us since ancient times. The National Institute of Health coined the term biofield therapy for this type of healing. It includes ancient Chinese therapies like acupuncture and auric healing. The treatments are based on the idea that the body has a biofield system like the circulatory, nervous, and lymphatic systems. Many academics and scientists are skeptical of biofield treatments and state they work because of the placebo effect. It is hard to believe that Jerri's 16-month-old child calmed down because of a placebo effect. Common types of spiritual healing include chakra healing, crystal/herbal remedies, breathwork, Reiki, Ayurveda, Chinese medicine, aromatherapy, meditation/visualization techniques, and so on. Whichever method of spiritual healing you use, it is a purposeful, systematic intervention performed by one or more people to help another person improve a condition they feel needs improving. As it becomes better understood, they have increasingly used its healing methods worldwide.

True spiritual healing is about facing, acknowledging, exploring, digesting, and accepting whatever we are going through. The idea is to eliminate the festering problem and immunize yourself from its effects on you. Think of it like this: if you had a horrific sore oozing blood and pus, you wouldn't achieve healing by closing your eyes and ignoring it. The pain and infection would still be there. If you put a bandage on it, it may or may not heal. The way to remedy that soreness is to face it, accept it, and find a way to alleviate your suffering and the right medicine to cure it. Spiritual healing is the same. It helps if you get to the roots of your issues to heal them.

Initially, the original spiritual healing was simply the laying on of hands or passing the hands over the body. During the past few years, auric healing has evolved into Reiki. Reiki supposedly links your spiritual energy with the energy of the Universe. It works through the realization that we are born with omniscient wisdom to heal and preserve life. All life is interconnected. Our basic skills, which our ancestors relied on, and we hardly use today, have been forgotten. We rely on modern medicine, which is fine, but spiritual healing can be an excellent adjunct to it.

Spiritual healing can keep us in balance with our spiritual essence rather than giving up the responsibility for our life and health to other people. Reiki is the catalyst for that to happen. Many people believe that a teacher will find you and guide you when you are ready to embrace Reiki's principles. It has become so well known that when people first hear about it, they accept it because it feels natural. We are spiritual people and recognize there is a ubiquitous energy force giving life to every organism in existence. We have known about this energy for thousands of years and have sought to develop ways to use it to heal and guide us on our journey to eternity. The Japanese call this energy Ki. It is known as Chi by the Chinese, Prana by many Asian cultures, and the breath of life, or simply spiritual energy, by most of the Western world.

We carry this energy in and around our bodies from our birth. It is like the energy of our soul. Science has proven its existence, and with Kirlian photography, we can see this energy that encompasses all living things. Ancient Eastern cultures have harnessed and applied this energy for healing for thousands of years. Many successful disciplines such as Reiki, Tai Chi, Feng Shui, Meditation, Yoga, and Acupuncture control and enhance the energy flow in and around the body. The energy itself is spiritual, pure, and has omniscient wisdom. Many spiritual people say that by practicing the discipline of Reiki, you regain your natural abilities to heal yourself and others, and the knowledge you need to lead a happier, more fulfilling life. Nature's life-giving energy is a great and wise teacher. By pursuing its wisdom through the practice of Reiki, you will supposedly grow to new heights of understanding, and life will flow at a more enjoyable and exciting pace. Remember always this life-giving energy is a gift from the Universe. Many people use it without knowing it.

When a child falls and hurts their knee, instinctively, they place their hand on the sore spot, and the pain is relieved as they unconsciously work with this energy to heal themselves. Likewise, a parent will kiss their child's hurt or injured limb and place their hand on it. Unknowingly, both the parent and the child are working unconsciously with this healing energy. The parent sends and channels the energy; the child receives and draws the energy. This incredible energy is free. There are no patents or copyrights attached. All you need is the desire and the discipline to attune yourself to the energy, and Reiki is a form of hands-on healing, with its origins in India and the East dating back many thousands of years to the time before Christ and Buddha. Reiki's original name, disciplines, and techniques are no longer with us because the traditional method of passing knowledge from generation to generation by word of mouth has allowed the original methods to become distorted many times.

Reiki is a two-syllable Japanese word meaning universal life force. Esoterically, Rei means spiritual consciousness, the omniscient wisdom from the higher self. Reiki is inbuilt intelligence that energizes the mind, body, and spirit. Reiki stimulates growth, health, life, and healing. When freely allowed to flow around the body, it can keep us alive and healthy for over 120 years. Unfortunately, bad habits and poor choices stifle the flow of Reiki. It is important to note that Reiki is indestructible. Even when we die and the life force leaves our body, it continues to exist as part of the Universe.

When the mind, body, and spirit are in harmony, the biological intelligence, which governs the body's resources and allows it to heal itself and function correctly, is intensified. Reiki is the key that unlocks the body's optimum capabilities. Seven major energy centers in the body control the flow of the universal life force. They are called the Chakras. Each chakra supplies energy to specific parts of the body. When they get blocked or clogged, the body becomes sick, and the energy flow becomes stymied. A complete Reiki treatment reopens the chakras and unblocks the flow of the universal life force around the body. A person will typically need four full treatments on four consecutive days to boost the flow of Reiki energy. These treatments will stimulate the body's immune system and natural healing abilities. Usually, the body will begin by cleansing itself of toxins. The body becomes re-balanced as the poisons get removed, and the healing begins.

Many cultures have developed techniques and disciplines that stimulate the flow of Ki energy around the body. However, Reiki is the easiest to learn and administer. The method is simple to master, with profound results. Historically, spiritual healing has been free for anyone to practice.

We are going through a terrific amount of tension throughout the world right now. If you are new at spiritual healing or have done it often, please be careful about who and when you practice it. Governments worldwide might forbid its practice and punish anyone who does it. Also, in turbulent times like this, the person you do it with could be one of those people who will turn on you and accuse you of harming them. Do exercises like these with people you trust and enjoy being around. Also, when a group gets together to practice exercises like Reiki, sometimes one person might say something like, "I don't feel anything." Or when you treat someone for the first time, they will say it isn't working. That is all right. Some people will reject what other people do just to reject it. The same people will swear they can't meditate, which is simply the art of focusing on one thing. Everyone enters a meditative state at night, either when they relax on the way to sleep or wake up. For some reason, they just don't want to accept what's going on. It has nothing to do with you. They just wasted a few minutes of your time. The practice helps you anyway.

Reiki healing is easy to perform. You can get excellent instruction on the internet. Reiki courses cost anywhere from $19.99 to $99.99, depending on how much you want to spend. It is a fundamental routine of aura healing. The first step is asking the person you work with to sit down or lie down. Next, you ground yourself. You ground yourself by relaxing, taking a few deep breaths, and possibly repeating a mantra or meditating for a minute or two. Not long. Then, starting with your hands comfortably spread apart, place them about an inch above your subject's head. There is a power point in the palm of your hand that radiates spiritual energy. When you place your hands about an inch apart and move them back and forth as if you are clapping without the final touch, you can feel the air between them. The atmosphere you feel is your aura, but the palms of your hands are like horns sending out streams of energy. This energy goes through your subject's aura and is like an ignition switch that starts the healing.

Slowly pass your hands over your subject's body while meditating and focus on sending them healing energy. When possible, place your hands on either side of their body, allowing you to send them more power. Move your hands slowly up and down their body, spending extra time above places they feel need more healing or places you sense need more healing. You can also softly place your hands on the body parts for which they want healing. After all, the term healing touch means healing done by touch.

THOUGHTS

- There are many ideas about the basis of the Universe
- Plato felt knowledge was the primary universal energy
- Energy is the fundamental material of the Universe
- Spiritual energy continually evolves and changes
- You are living, evolving spiritual energy
- Humankind has lived on Earth for at least 200,000 years
- Hospitals now use Healing Touch
- Science recognizes the existence of the human aura
- Reiki is a natural form of healing

CHAPTER 15
YOU ARE WHOLE

THINK BACK TO WHEN YOU WERE A CHILD. MAYBE YOU lived with two parents. Perhaps you were raised in an orphanage. Possibly your grandparents, an aunt, or even an older sibling may have brought you up. Or you were an only child. It doesn't matter who you lived with as a child; you still spent time as a young person affected by people who strongly influenced your life. The people or person who took responsibility for helping you grow up also had people, or a person, responsible for helping them grow up. It is doubtful anybody helping anybody grow up had any training that would make them competent in how to help someone grow up to be a responsible adult.

Some children start out as rotten, cruel, mean, absolutely horrible people. Other children start out as gentle, caring, loving, and absolutely wonderful people. An old story goes like this: All little girls are born with 10,000 angels on their shoulders, and all little boys are born with 10,000 devils. Every day of their lives, one little angel jumps off the shoulders of the little girl it lives on and onto a little boy's shoulders. Also, every day of their lives, one little devil jumps off the little boy's shoulders and onto a little girl's shoulders. So, at the closing days of their lives, the old lady has 10,000 devils on her shoulders, and the old man has 10,000 angels on his shoulders.

It is unclear where that story came from or who first wrote it, but there is a point we can consider. Every one of us experiences a massive amount of change as we go through life. When we are first born, we bring certain traits along with us. While we spend time on Earth, we can manifest a life of abundance, love, happiness, and harmony or disaster, hatred, melancholy, and pain. It is up to us to manifest our own life because we have free will. As spiritual beings, we have control over how we react to the energies of the Universe that constantly bombard us. Some fundamental energies are good, and others are not so good. The fact is that it is probable the person, or people, who brought you into this world and raised you had no training about how to help you become a perfect adult. All thoughts, words, actions, and emotions are contagious. Chances are you picked up many of your ways of thinking and acting from your parents, siblings, or other children with whom you associated. Or the way they acted repelled you in such a way that caused you to behave the opposite of them. Either way, they had a tremendous effect on how you behave today. It is normal for brothers to act the opposite of each other. It is the same with sisters.

As a child, you found yourself in a new place where you often learned new stuff. You learned how to speak the language other people around you spoke, and you were living because of the care of the people or person who took care of you. You may have helped raise your siblings, or they may have helped raise you. You may have been an only child, and you may have had a helicopter mother, a lady who hovered over you and protected you from any possibility of being harmed. As you grew up, you formed the beliefs and characteristics that would create your adult life.

Then, as an adult, you discovered you had to learn new ways of surviving. You no longer had parents or older siblings to deal with and on which to depend. Some people immediately settle down to one job and do nothing creative or anything to bring change into their lives for the rest of their lives. They live rather boring adult lives until they pass away. But they go through change anyway because of the way others treat them. After reaching adulthood, certain people question everything they know. They look inward and decide what they learned as a young person wasn't right. They meet new people, make new friends, and have new challenges to face. They will make drastic changes like divorcing their mate, quitting their job, changing their religious affiliations or beliefs, spiritual views, and going back to school.

These feelings and thoughts that things aren't suitable can begin in childhood, but remain repressed until the person is older and places a higher value on themselves. Wilber felt at 12 years old that he was in the wrong place. He didn't understand what it was, but he thought he needed to be somewhere else and didn't know where. He joined the army soon after graduating from high school. After he served his boot camp, his first eight weeks in the military, he married his high school sweetheart. Wilbur did well in the army, but spent most of his time away from home while training with his army unit. After six years and two children, he felt he needed a civilian job, so he left the army and moved to a state far away from his original family. His marriage wasn't happy, but he had two children and felt it was wrong to leave his wife. One of Wilbur's major complaints was that his wife spent too much money. Wilber was relatively frugal and said his wife spent a little more money every month than he ever earned. His debt was on an ever-increasing upward curve.

When Wilber was 38 years old, his father died, and Wilber went back home to the funeral. He had always visited his family at least once a year. On this visit, he noticed how well his wife got along with the rest of his family. He appreciated that fact, but saw how much she acted like they did. He said they all acted like they were better than anyone else, and he was stupid. Wilbur said his relatives and wife treated him like a village idiot and that he would be nothing without her. By this time, Wilber was successful and had developed a great deal of self-confidence. He soon felt he had never left home, and it was people like his wife he should not be around. He then told his wife that she should treat him better or that he would leave. Nothing changed, and after four more years, he talked her into seeing a marriage counselor.

They went to see the marriage counselor, and the counselor asked Wilbur to discuss his complaints first. Wilbur started talking about why he was unhappy with the marriage and, after only being interrupted with questions and other remarks a few times, stopped talking 45 minutes later. After a brief silence, the counselor told Wilber that since he had spoken for so long, it would be good to wait until the next meeting to hear the wife's side of the story. Wilbur quickly agreed because he was weary after letting his dissatisfaction out. The next meeting never came. His wife refused to go back and tell her side. Wilbur waited for the next meeting for two months, but when it didn't happen, he left. Since his children were grown, he moved from the house to another city and looked for a new job. It took him several weeks to get the new job, and he was very low on money, but he got along okay. He sent money to his wife for about six months and then stopped because he barely made enough money to survive. He didn't want to get the divorce because his father had taught that marriage is a lifelong commitment and if you get married, you have to live with your decision, or you are a terrible person.

He very much wanted his wife to divorce him. About a year later, after he stopped sending his wife money because he didn't have any, she divorced him. Her family was wealthy, and they had always lorded their wealth over him about how much richer they were than him. After the marriage ended, Wilbur was soon attending meetings with spiritual people. He felt a kinship with people interested in meditating and doing things like having seances and doing psychic fairs. He meditates every day now. His children are now married. His only girl is a born-again Christian, and his two sons don't bother with anything to do with religion. Looking back at his life, he said, "Most of my life, I thought I had to leave the place I lived before I could find myself. I left home when I was young to get away. I didn't get away. When I got married, I took the place I knew I had to get away from with me. But it was the people I associated with who I needed to leave. When I finally left my marriage and moved to another city, I left home, and I could become myself. It took me a couple of years to find myself, but I did." Wilber and his ex-wife eventually found new mates and found new opportunities for happiness.

Wilbur's story is typical of many spiritual people. Their parents barely reached adulthood when they had children and didn't know what they were doing. They went to school and saw how their elders function and believed that's how they should behave. They copied the behavior in their own manner. Very few children sit down and analyze what their life is about and how to make the most progress while they live on Earth. Their parents didn't bother to look inward or outward to learn what living was all about. They did whatever they believed would get them from the present day to the next day.

Many spiritual people have to unlearn what they learned as a child, and there are so few of us that it's challenging to find anyone who will help us along. The number of admittedly spiritual people is increasing, and as we continue to grow, we will become more accessible, and it will be easier to accept one's spirituality. Think of it this way. We know the Universe is one humongous entity of energy, being, brain, or whatever you want to call it. The Universe is energy. Science proved this over a hundred years ago when Albert Einstein produced the proof that matter and energy are the same, only different emanations of the same material. When you break that material down to its most natural basis, it turns into Qui, spiritual energy, the breath of life, or whatever you want to call it. It is the substance that fills the entire universe. It is the substance of eternal life.

During the past 100 years, many scientists have echoed the idea that all matter contains a substance called information. Occasionally, they suggest information is more fundamental than matter, energy, space, and time. Physicist John Wheeler encapsulates what many physicists believe: "that tangible physical reality. . . is ultimately made from information." In the book *Information and the Nature of Reality,* Paul Davies claims that information "occupies the ontological basement." It is not about something. It is itself something. No matter what the scientists say, even if they admit that knowledge or information is universal, we all have innate thoughts that point in the direction we receive information from the universe. In philosophy and psychology, an innate idea is knowledge, or a concept considered universal to all humanity; it is something people are born with rather than learned through experience. Examples of innate knowledge are birds instinctively knowing how to build nests, and horses knowing how to stand up and walk immediately after birth. It is common for parents and mothers, especially, to feel it when their children experience trauma. It is a psychic thing.

When you break down all of this complicated jargon, it appears to signify that we, as humans, are basically our thoughts. Our soul, composed of fundamental spiritual energy, spreads throughout our bodies and into our auras. It picks up information from the primary spiritual energy of the Universe, other spiritual people, and everything else it encounters. We hear things that bring us information, and we see, feel, dream, touch, experience, and innately absorb knowledge. The activity of absorbing new knowledge or information is a continuous experience. The beauty of our spiritual soul that controls our bodies' feelings, moods, thoughts, and activities is that it always creates our future life. The Universe contains spiritual, subtle, or what people call Qui energy. This energy is like stem cells in the human body, as they can form any other energy. A basic form of energy produced by spiritual energy is soul energy. Soul energy attracts or develops physical energy for bodies to use. Our bodies, in turn, experience feelings from what we touch, hear, and speak. Your soul experiences these sounds and emotions through your thoughts. You feel your thoughts mainly in your head and your solar plexus, but you can feel them in every part of your body.

Only You Can Manifest Your Future

We don't know why this exquisite creature, which we call God, Source, or the Universe, allows us to form our human body and spend time on earth. We know we have free will and can manifest whatever we want while we exist here. Many self-help books and gurus claim it is easy to turn your life around if you are unhappy or not pleased with it. But it is difficult and can take years of effort. What they tell you to do works, and sometimes it works quickly. Other times it doesn't work because whoever is changing their life quits too soon. You either brought happiness, unhappiness, or whatever you wanted to change with you as karma, or you developed it as a child. If it is karma, it may have taken more than one lifetime to develop. We know we continually manifest our future, so we must consciously continue to manifest our future until the change takes place. The first thing you need to do is decide what kind of person you want to be. You can decide what you want your friends to be like, how other people treat you, and what you wish your future mate will look like and act like. Describing what you want your life to be like will probably take some deep thought. Next, it is essential to think up the affirmations, visualizations, and possible journaling what you plan to do.

Now that you have decided who you want to become and how you will do it, you must follow through and do it until your plan for your future life develops. Your subconscious thoughts will often work against you because they create a comfort zone in how you presently act. You may start acting how you want, and attracting the people you want in your life, and believe you accomplished your goal, but then have a setback. You suddenly revert to your old self without noticing it. You may have to do affirming, manifesting, visualizing, and journaling for many months to accomplish your goal. But remember, you are a spiritual being with free will. You are one part of an ever-changing, beautiful spiritual essence and can contribute to that change in any way you want. You handle your body's thoughts, feelings, and activities. No one but you can plan your future but yourself. You will encounter many people who want you to change your life or make you stay the same as you are, but they can only affect you with your consent.

While you focus on your future, see yourself as the best person you can be. Ask yourself what kind of people you want to attract. How do you want people to treat you? Where do you plan to live? There are all kinds of questions you can ask yourself. Intentionally practice being the person you want to become. You are always practicing becoming your future person just by being you.

The feeling of love, as long as it feels good, improves your life in every way. When you are close to someone and feel bad for them, that is not love; it is empathy. How you perceive the present moment of your life determines your state of love. How you feel, think, act, and react to whatever life presents you at this moment, right now, decides your state of love. Living in a state of love comes from living in the now and with the courage to feel loved. It comes with your ability to be open-minded and flexible. It's about connection, trust, sharing, collaboration support, inner peace, and including others. All of this comes from your soul, and it allows your soul to direct and inform your life. Living in a state of love, having the feeling of love ingrained deep in every cell of your being, is not about being naïve about love. By the time you reach the point where love is a natural mode of living, you probably have had more than one relationship with other people. It's possible you have hurt others and have been hurt by others. These experiences teach you to set boundaries for how you allow others to treat you and guidelines for how you treat others. You will feel trepidation, fear, discomfort, or other negative emotions you will recognize as a warning from people not interested in treating you with respect. These feelings are navigational tools. They tell you who to associate with and who to avoid. Being filled with spiritual love, you will become a shining light that attracts people who want to love and be loved. Good for you.

Back in the day, 200,000 years ago, no one considered the importance of love in a relationship. People lived together in small groups, and the group leader chose whoever he wanted for his mate. She would have a child, and the group would slowly grow until it became a tribe. There weren't any social rules about how people should treat each other or mate. It was a happenstance type of thing. It was natural, and humankind instinctively wanted to bring more souls to Earth. Love wasn't an essential part of finding a mate until reasonably recently. We had periods where the parents picked the partners, and the potential lovers' wealth determined the coupling. We even had periods where the male was supposed to rescue the damsel in distress or save her from becoming an old maid.

The most limiting aspect of the belief about love is that you can only love one person at a time. As we previously described, there are many so-called types of love, but most are selfish feelings for oneself. Spiritual love is open, friendly, and beneficial for all parties involved. You can be the instigator of this type of love. It all comes when you develop the courage to be it and do it. It can be terrifying. If they expose their loving nature, most people feel others will take advantage of their goodness. Very few people will reveal their unloving nature. Spiritual people who abide by their boundaries about how people treat them have no trouble with people taking advantage of their loving kindness. Have you ever walked down the street smiling at people to see how many of them would smile back at you? My friend Paul did. He was downtown and started smiling at people. He smiled at 25 people, and 22 smiled back at him. Paul said he wasn't sure the people who didn't return his smile saw him. They were all people Paul didn't know, but they willingly returned his smile. A smile is a universal sign of friendship, and the people Paul smiled at seemed happy to accept Paul's smile.

Others have criticized and mocked people outside the standard religious tradition for years. It is time for spiritual people to open up about their understanding of our spiritual selves. There is room for many beliefs, and they are all right. From this moment on, allow yourself to shine as the beautiful spiritual creature you are. Meanwhile, please check for my other books, podcasts, and a blog on the internet where you can make comments and ask questions at https://walterbroach.com. And please remember that you are a wonderful human being.

THOUGHTS

- People raise children while still children
- We experience change throughout life
- We bring many traits with us when we are born
- Adults often unlearn what they learned as children
- Spiritual energy is the substance of eternal life
- You can feel your thoughts throughout your body
- Only you can manifest your future
- Dare to glow and dare to grow
- There is room for many beliefs
- Dare to be your best self

ABOUT THE AUTHOR

CURIOSITY ABOUT THE WHEREABOUTS OF ONE'S SOUL HAS spurred Walter Broach's interest in metaphysics since he was a child. People from many countries have widely praised and accepted his books *About Spiritual Energy* and *Spiritual Energy Explained.* Before writing books, he spent years as a public library director, organized many groups to study metaphysical phenomena, and not only practiced giving psychic readings, but taught people how to give readings themselves. He has taken part in auric and Reiki healings and helped many people experience past life regressions.

Walter is 86 years old and lives in Broken Arrow, Oklahoma, with his beautiful wife, Ellen. They have six happy and successful children between them scattered throughout the United States. He is perhaps the world's foremost proponent that every human being is a spirit or soul walking around in a physical body. Walter enjoys discussing everything about Ki, another name for psychic or spiritual energy. He has researched the subject for over 50 years. He has also performed many past life regressions, taken part in psychic fairs, and taught such subjects as Reiki and auric healing. His writing style is thorough, relaxed, and conversational. Expect to enjoy everything he writes. Either add this book to your spiritual collection or buy it now and make it your first one.